WHEN WOMEN CHOOSE TO BE SINGLE

Rita Robinson

Newcastle Publishing Co., Inc.
North Hollywood, California
1991

Copyright © 1992 by Rita Robinson
All rights reserved.
ISBN 0-87877-170-0

Cover design by Michele Lanci-Altomare

No part of this book may be reproduced in any form without the expressed written consent of the publisher, except by a reviewer, who may quote brief passages in connection with a review.

FIRST EDITION
A NEWCASTLE BOOK
First printing 1992
10 9 8 7 6 5 4 3 2
Printed in the United States of America

For
DANA BROOKINS

courage and laughter

Contents

Acknowledgments vii

Introduction ix

I   Sometimes I Do Dishes at 2 A.M. 1
      There Is No Heathcliff   10

II   Our Place in History 11
      Present Pulses and Past Pundits   11
      Future Foibles   24

III   The Advantages of Money 27

IV   Street Smarts, or Down with Discrimination   41
      What Discrimination?   41
      Discrimination and Women's Health   46
      Living in the Here and Now   52

V   How to Be a Bitch and Other Self-Esteem Boosters 55
      You're Not Getting Older, You're Getting Bitchier   62
      They Should Have Bitched Instead   63

VI   AIDS and Other Sex-Busters 69

VII   Loneliness, Depression, and Other Normalities Like Friends and Celebrations   87
      Loneliness   87

Some Tips for Avoiding Loneliness   93
Friends   95
Celebrate   104
Handling Holiday Guilt   108
Depression   111

VIII   Tips and Tricks to Staying Healthy 115
Mind over Matter   115
Seven Health-Boosters for Tip-Top
   Shape   120
Protecting Your Cardiovascular
   System   131
Bouncing Back from Pain and Strain   140
Two Shadowy Words   145

IX   Out and About 149
The Restaurant Business   149
Peregrinations   158

X   Epilogue 169

Bibliography 177

Acknowledgments

I'd like to thank the following people for giving their time and insights which went into the making of this book: Gregory Adam, Mara Adelman, Pat Allen, Russell Archuleta, Elizabeth Bacon, Marshall Becker, Lee Berk, Kathryn Black, Harold Bloomfield, Walter Brackelmans, Don Brenneis, Carlfred Broderick, Dana Brookins, Barbara Cambridge, Robert Carney, Margaret Chesney, Joe Citro, Deborah Cohen, Thomas F. Coleman, Elizabeth Corson, De Creasy, Theresa Crenshaw, Barbara Cunningham, Ruth Dever, Marjory Stoneman-Douglas, Haila Dyrness, Sharon Richardson, Morris Egert, Marilyn Essex, Richard Fitzgibbons, Patricia Fleming, Georgie Anne Geyer, Rick Gibbony, Janet Giele, Sherri Grasmuck, Elizabeth Grauerholz, Laurence Grimm, Theodore Groat, Nancy Hardy, Aileen Haskell, Nick Hill, Paul Hilsdale, Thomas B. Holman, Victoria Howard, Larry Jamner, Lewis Judd, Aaron Katcher, Rebecca Kuzins, Karl Landis, Lois Langland, Marcia Lasswell, Jerry Lee, Dorothy Macy, Carol Mauro, Glenna McAnish, Lynn Miller, Milton Miller, Val Neilson, Linda Olsen, Audrey Phillips, David Phillips, Estelle Ramey, Arlene Saluter, Stormy Sandquist, Martin Barry Schlosser, Lorraine Shannon, Graham B. Spanier, Jan Stankas, Rege Stewart, Meier J. Stampfer, Shelley Taylor, Irene M. Thorelli, Adam Tihany, Howard E. Tinsley, Sharlene Wang, Myron L. Weisfeldt, Murray Wexler, Peter Wilson, Betty Wold, Sandra Yates.

Introduction

Living single frees the spirit. You're on your own, kiddo, and if you have the guts to ride it out, your life will be so full of adventure that you might feel sorry for your married friends.

Your single status takes on greater meaning, adventure, satisfaction and joy if it is a mind set somewhere between enjoying the company of intelligent, enlightened men and women and consciously choosing to live on your own. Well-adjusted single women aren't looking for lifemates, and this leaves them free to absorb the energy around them and turn on to life as never before. If they do decide to live with a man, they're doing so for all the right reasons rather than out of a need to feel complete.

Being single by choice doesn't mean that you grin and bear it. The single women I'm writing about don't worry about meeting men. If they happen to, fine, but in the meantime they're busy living, not just planning their lives. That's why healthy singles are so satisfied with life. They're not on the prowl, but their libidos aren't dead either.

Psychiatrist Harold Bloomfield, M.D., author of *Lifemates: The Love Fitness Program for a Lasting Relationship*, and successfully married to his coauthor, therapist Sirah Vettese, told me that although most research has found that the happily married career woman has the greatest sense of well-being, he believes that a well-adjusted single woman is even better off than her married sister.

"For a person to be single and healthy in our society requires the greatest self-esteem of anyone," he says. If single women have that particular brand of self-esteem, he adds, "then they're obviously quite happy."

Bloomfield also acknowledges what others in the psychotherapeutic community are admitting—that until recently, the mental-health field has been biased against single women. It has led female patients to believe that if they're not in some sort of a relationship, then something must be wrong with them, and that when they are "righted" they will be able to find a compatible mate and enjoy a long-lasting relationship.

With newer research and the growth in the number of singles, however, especially in the past 30 years, the stereotype of the "sicko single" is changing.

Janet Cockrum and Priscilla White write in the professional journal *Family Relations* that in 1957 "failure to marry was viewed as a pathology, but by the mid-seventies was seen only as a potential mechanism for increasing one's happiness."

Estelle Ramey, M.D., professor emeritus at Georgetown University School of Medicine in Washington, D.C., and a worldwide lecturer, states flatly that single women outlive married women and both single and married men. "It's interesting that even in the days when single women were regarded as spinsters who had nothing but a cat, and society held a pitying contempt for Old Aunt Agnes, they were still living the longest of anyone."

This myth—that those in stable relationships live the longest—has been perpetuated by the medical establishment because until the 1980s nearly all research was conducted on men. And it's true that single men have the worst health profiles.

The myths continue until you question the statistics. A recent study at the University of San Francisco led to newspaper headlines that read, "Death Risk High for Singles." When you look at the research itself, it showed that 23 percent of single men died during a given time, compared to 11 percent of married men. But only 7 percent of single women died during that time. The single women studied were low income and far fewer in number than the men studied. Not surprisingly, the study failed to report whether the single women studied were unmarried by choice and happy with that decision, or still skulking around, desperate to find a man because they were unable to support themselves adequately or because they felt incomplete as singles.

Growing numbers of women are choosing to be single for a variety of reasons. They're not hiding behind the old excuse that there aren't enough men to go around. And they're not worried that society will accuse them of having something emotionally or physically wrong with themselves.

Since 1970, the proportion of women 25 to 29 who have never married has tripled, according to U.S. Census Bureau figures. For all age groups, twice as many women choose to be single today as they did 20 years ago.

New research discussed in later chapters reveals why more women are electing to be single, and the major reason is that women simply have more choices today. Once women have achieved economic independence—not wealth but *independence*—they become more selective about how and with whom (if anyone) they want to live their lives.

There are several categories of single women: never married, divorced, and widowed. They don't necessarily exclude men from their lives. Many single women simply prefer living on their own. Research shows that men on their own don't fare well. Women, on the other hand, thrive, both mentally and physically. In order to thrive, they have taken responsibility for their choices, stopped whining and gotten on with life. If certain situations are unfair to singles, then it's up to them to take action for change (see chapter 4).

The women who speak on the following pages have chosen not to marry or remarry for periods ranging from three years to a lifetime. Many have never given a thought to the success of their chosen way of living, and many others are well aware that they couldn't have lived their lives as richly had they chosen differently.

During my interview with columnist and foreign correspondent Georgie Anne Geyer a few years ago, following her return from South America, she talked briefly about being single. She acknowledged that she couldn't have been as successful or as happy doing the kind of work she did had she been married. She said she loved men, but knew early on that her life of travel and work wouldn't be compatible with marriage.

On the other hand, some women choose to be single for several years and then decide they want to live with someone.

Peggy W., in her early 40s and a partner in a West Coast bookkeeping service, had been single for eight years and wasn't looking for a husband. "Suddenly," as she described it, she felt the need to live with someone. She's putting as much energy into finding a mate as she now puts into her successful business.

Jacqueline Simenauer, co-author of *Singles: The New Americans*, 1982, told me that she had been a committed single, but when she decided it was time to marry, she set about in earnest to find a good husband. She didn't believe in setting her sights low enough to make it easy. She and several other single career women decided to throw a once-a-month party replete with all the trappings of a celebration. Each donated $40 toward food and entertainment and each invited an eligible bachelor on the ground that they were "celebrating" someone's promotion or transfer. Through the months they met many eligible men and all but one of them eventually married someone they had met at the parties. Simenauer married a classical musician—he's enlightened, mature, well-traveled and well-read.

It's Simenauer's belief that if you're serious about something, be it singleness or finding a mate, then you don't dilly-dally. Know what you want and go after it, she advises. The desire to be single can change, as it did for her, and for women like Peggy W. Acknowledging and acting upon that change is healthy.

Neither Georgie Anne nor the women I've interviewed, nor I myself, advocate singlehood over marriage. That would be like arguing whether eggs are better fried or scrambled. The choice is one of personal taste, which depends on where you're at in your life; whether or not you feel good about yourself; how indoctrinated you've been by society's expectations (remember, some of society's expectations are self-induced); and how good you are at thumbing your nose at convention and taking your own bows or blame.

Most of us who are truly enjoying our lives as singles know that not living as a couple is just one more choice in our multiethnic, ecumenical, variegated society. It's our choice—not our fate. Many of us have been married, have lived with men in relationships, and continue to love men. But we've chosen to live our day-to-day lives on our own.

This book is not your usual tome on how to snag a man. Nor is it a put-down of those who choose marriage. It's a celebration of single women who delight in being who and what they are despite society's discrimination, stereotyping and bias, and despite our own normal insecurities.

This book is for single women who are convinced that their lives are full without permanent relationships. It's also for those less-secure women who don't feel complete without a man. For them, the book might give some insights into how they can meet themselves and learn to like the person they've found.

I

Sometimes I Do Dishes at 2 A.M.

"I dated a doctor for a while and the first time he came to my apartment he walked through every room, inspected my art work, the furnishings and how everything was arranged," says Glenna McAnish, 54. "Then he said, 'You'll never marry again. You'll never find a man who can give you the things you have given yourself.'

"I was freshly divorced and his comment shocked me, but it was true," she goes on. "If I want to play the piano at midnight, I can. And that's not selfish. I suppose my piano could go in another room but I like it in the living room. If there were a man in the house, he'd want to watch television in that room and he'd be miffed if I wouldn't watch it with him."

McAnish has the black hair and dark, prankish eyes of the Irish. Her life has been as colorful as her personality, with euphoric highs and desperate lows. It's obvious from the moment you meet her that a great sense of humor has carried her through the turmoil she's faced, including marriage at an early age, divorce, remarriage, another divorce, as well as raising three young children by herself, and serious financial problems when she found herself on disability at 52 following an automobile accident in which her best friend was killed. McAnish suffered slight brain damage, but is recovering. When I interviewed her less than two years after the accident, she was working at a gift shop in the mountain resort town of Big Bear, California, and the owners had just put her in charge of a new shop they'd opened in another mountain community.

A statement she made sums up the independent attitude of many single women, especially those who were previously married. "Sometimes I do dishes at 2 A.M.," she said with a grin. "And sometimes I hide the dirty ones."

Like McAnish, many single women delight in their freedom, no matter where it takes them. This is what a few of them have to say about their independence:

—"A person can't do as much if they're taking care of another person." Marjory Stoneman-Douglas, 100, author and environmentalist.

—"Freedom comes before money." Rebecca Kuzins, 40, journalist.

—"Being single can be fun. It's not just being single. It's a whole attitude about being single." Barbara Cambridge, around 50, sociologist.

—"I've always insisted on paying my own way. One man was old-schoolish and said it embarrassed him. So I told him on the way into a restaurant, 'No problem. I'll give you the money before we go in.'" Dorothy L. Macy, 80, retired union executive.

—"Other people expect you to have certain things done at certain times and I'm at a point in my life where if I want to throw my stuff on the floor, I'm going to throw my stuff on the floor, and pick it up when I want to." De Creasy, 33, career counselor for disabled students.

—"When women are on their own, there's simply one

less person to take care of." Sherri Grasmuck, around 30, sociologist.
— "Women who really enjoy being single, and who do well with it, are women who have their own identity." Rege Stewart, M.D., psychiatrist.
— "If they want to do something, single women don't have to ask permission." Marcia Lasswell, late 70s, psychologist.
— "The greatest thing about being single is that you have more options. You develop your own taste. You don't have to compromise. I think even when I was married, I was a married single." Elizabeth Bacon, 42, newspaper editor.
— "I saw this woman on TV and she said she kissed her car every morning. I can understand her. Ten years ago, I would have said I like being single because I had discovered that I could take care of myself. Now it's down to more nitty-gritty things. I get into a car that *I* bought. My money goes into the slot machines. That's my house I paid for." Dana Brookins, 60, writer and English professor.
— "Women who choose to be single frequently feel that love of learning and intellectual stimulation are greater attractions than marriage." Lois Langland, 71, professor of psychology.
— "Guess I love me too much to get bored." Audrey Phillips, 87, retired real estate agent.

Most of the women interviewed for this book, and who made these statements, were married at one time.

Some, but not all, of the women who have never been married say they might consider it if the right man presented himself, but they don't believe it's likely they will meet a man who meets their expectations. They are career women with a multitude of interests, who date, but who say the men in their lives don't come up to their standards for lifetime commitments. One says her biological clock has "damn well ticked out." Another is considering surrogate motherhood.

You could say that some women have painted themselves into a corner. They have delayed marriage, become well educated and can't find men who can offer them what they now expect. Mara Adelman, a professor of communication at Northwestern University, Illinois, says, "We used to look at men and judge them compared to other men. Women looked for appropriate age, assets, income, education and worldliness. But we have become more like men, so now our comparisons are with ourselves."

Adelman, who is single, acknowledges that she hasn't resolved feelings about her own single status. "I go up and down on my roller coaster, which suggests my singleness isn't completely resolved. I have periods during which the idea of being without a mate, or without intimacy (since to me intimacy doesn't mean a full-time live-in), makes me really wonder.

"Some women celebrate singlehood, but I wonder if that celebration is because they still perceive options. They can still imagine themselves dating single men. These options become diminished over time until you know that you are going to be single forever. I've had to work that through myself. Is mine a forced choice or a voluntary one?"

Adelman believes we need to understand that as singles we'll be going through these emotional stages, but that we need to remember: We own our singleness.

Theodore Groat, a sociologist at Bowling Green State University in Ohio, gives another view: "People justify their situation in life and come to the conclusion that it is best for them. So they construct a social reality in their own minds that makes things seem more palatable. If you are, say, 60 or older, there are so many more women than men that it's demographically impossible to remarry. That being the case, there should then be a subculture of people saying they are better off not being married."

Some sociologists and psychologists agree that we do rationalize, but not always the same way. "Singles have an image of what they see themselves as, and then they perceive what they would be like if they were married. Maybe they base that image on a former marriage or what their friends are going through, and they make a conscious choice. They may be having a relationship, but still they have no intention of being married because they have an image of themselves as being single, and they're going on with their lives as they choose," says Barbara Cambridge, a sociologist at University of Texas Southwestern Medical Center at Dallas. She was widowed when her children were young and she has never remarried.

She also says, "It's my freedom to be who I am and to be what God has created me to be and do on this planet. I'm more in touch with that everyday. There are things for me to do that I haven't yet done. I want to see and do for as long as I can and not just take up space on this planet. I think if you choose to be single and are okay with it, and believe in yourself, it can be wonderful."

Some of the women quoted previously and who were once married, made conscious choices before they were 40 to remain single and never marry again. None regrets that decision.

There are instances, however, when a committed single can have a change of heart. Carol Mauro, executive editor at *Longevity* magazine, until she turned 40 had been perfectly content with her life as a single. "I'd had good success in my career. I'd proven myself. Of course, you could turn that around and say I hadn't proved myself in marriage."

Mauro was married in 1990. "He literally swept me off my feet. I'd known him for a long time and at one point he came back into my life. He pursued me with flowers and the whole bit. And I'm completely happy. I finally decided I was lonely, and that work wasn't everything."

Mauro believes that if she had been in an unsuccessful marriage previously, she might not have been so enthusiastic about such a commitment.

Betty Wold of Gore, Oklahoma, now 70, was divorced in her early 60s. She says that, had she felt as secure in her marriage as she does as a single person, she may have liked her marriage better or might have been willing to try it again. "I tell my kids not to get married unless they think that being married is going to be better than being single."

Psychologist Marcia Lasswell, an instructor at both the University of Southern California and California State University, Pomona, says there are other reasons not to marry. "Many single women say they don't want to take care of a man, particularly if they are older," she says. "They grew up with men of the same age who are traditional and who want to be taken care of. These women are concerned that if they take care of a man, they'll have to submerge their own individuality. They have found that they love their freedom. They don't ever want to have to ask permission for anything again.

"Women in careers or who at least have satisfying work

and have a circle of friends and have learned to navigate in the world aren't willing to give up their independence until the absolutely perfect man comes along. They aren't out seeking. They're quite content," says Lasswell. "Women who are constantly looking don't know how to get involved. They're not good at networking and keeping friendships. One of my clients said the other day, 'It takes a very, very good man to be better than no man at all.' What she was really saying was, 'I don't want to get married again because men don't want their mates to have anything more important than themselves.' They want the woman to be available for them even if she is working. Women who have careers or a variety of interests would rather not be bothered."

Victoria Howard, a 45-year-old California artist, recently attended the funeral of a friend. The deceased happened to be the sister of a man Howard had been engaged to at the age of 21, but she had decided not to marry him. She said it was strange talking to him at the funeral—as if their relationship had happened in another lifetime. At one point in her life, she taught sign language to deaf children. But she gave that career up five years ago, attended art school for three years, and just got back from Paris. Now she is setting up a studio loft in Los Angeles.

"It has always been my choice not to marry," she says. "I've had 14 proposals, but have always been more interested in my work," she says.

Howard, like many women I interviewed, is afraid of losing her autonomy. "I get very involved in a man and then I get insecure and then I stop my work. When I find myself unproductive, I get depressed."

Many women admit that when they are in a relationship

with a man they tend to lose their own identity. They take a back seat to a man, so as to not overshadow him.

But Howard says, "Truthfully, I've met few men I really respect. I've lived with two different men, but I'm not sure I ever committed to anybody. It's a tradeoff. When I get down, I have to look around and pat myself on the back."

Women are or become single and stay single for a variety of reasons. Some who have been married say they would never, under any circumstances, marry again. Others say they would if the right man came along. They just don't believe he ever will, so they've planned their lives to not include men. Many would, and do, have loving relationships with men, but they won't live with them.

"Women of all ages may be longing for a man, but they're not prepared to settle for what's available," says sociologist Sherri Grasmuck, head of women's studies at Temple University. You can say that marriage doesn't serve women as well as it serves men, without saying necessarily that women don't want to be married. Both sexes often don't want to get married, and that's quite evident from our divorce rate. The problem is, people have been socialized to think that marriage is an end to all their problems."

The decision to marry or to stay single isn't a simple one. Both options involve a multitute of reasons and social prices. As women become more entrenched in the work force, the need for someone to take care of them diminishes. But then other needs come into play.

"Women feel a genuine yearning for human companionship, a need that you associate with the desire to marry," says Grasmuck. "They're wanting that kind of human companionship. They're not needing someone to take care of them. They don't need someone just to bring home the bacon. So they're much freer to talk about what they want and to say, 'Yes, I'm needy, but what I want is love.' Women can say, 'I want a lover,' and they're comfortable with that. Men are just as desperate for that kind of companionship, but they haven't been socialized to admit it."

A single man told me he believed that fear may play a part in some women's not wanting to marry. I asked him to explain the type of fear he was talking about and he said, "Well, the fear of failure again if they've already been divorced."

In a sense I have to agree with him, but not entirely. I'm sure there are women who don't remarry because they were somehow hurt by what they went through in a previous marriage. But I believe it's much more likely that the fear is one of giving up independence.

Kathryn Black, a psychology professor at Purdue University in Indiana, maintains that most women would prefer to be in a good romantic relationship, but it's tough to find one as fewer women are inclined to lower their sights. Adding to the dilemma is the shortage of men in some age groups. That makes it doubly tough to find a man who meets the higher standards of today's educated and career-minded woman.

"I see a lot of young women, 21 to 25, who say they aren't ready to marry yet," says Black. "But very few of them would say they intend never to marry, unless they have been burned and don't want to try it again."

Several conclusions arise from the foregoing discussions: Women have a variety of reasons for staying single. The more education a woman has, or the more interesting and well-paying her career, the less need she has to marry. The more educated a woman, and the more career-minded she is, the harder it is to find a man who is her equal.

There Is No Heathcliff

Author and English professor Dana Brookins recently told me about a tongue-in-cheek organization called the TINH club, which stands for "There Is No Heathcliff."

About 15 years ago she was in the company of three others when the discussion fell to the lack of virtue in men.

All were fans of Emily Brontë's *Wuthering Heights*, and of Sir Laurence Olivier, who played Heathcliff in the movie version. All thought that Heathcliff had the kind of virtue they were talking about. Today Brookins says, "Looking at it now, who would want the kind of devotion he personified?"

Val Neilson, a 38-year-old San Francisco career woman who's been divorced for several years, says she'd be happy to meet a man she'd be compatible with, but she once tried a video-dating service and viewed the tape she made of herself. She thought, "Why do I need a man? I'm everything I'm looking for."

Perhaps Neilson felt then what healthy single women have known all along: I *have* met Heathcliff and he is me.

II

Our Place in History

Present Pulses and Past Pundits

Audrey Phillips's second husband died when she was 38. Phillips came close to marrying three or four times after he died, but always balked because she didn't want to give up her freedom and independence. For most of her life she held a good job and didn't need the financial security some men give to women.

Audrey believes it's easier to be single today than it was when she started out. "Single women of my generation had to be circumspect," she says. "Tongues wagged if you saw too much of a man, or went with too many men, or acted like you were having too much fun." Complicating life was the fact that in general the men of her day didn't appreciate independent women. For the most part, today's young men don't look on single women as having descended from another planet. Many of them even like independent, self-sufficient women. To call these men a majority, however, might be stretching the truth.

Attitudes do change, sometimes purely because of economics. Few families could survive today on one paycheck, so it has become necessary to accept women who work. But wait! Women have always worked. Widows and unmarrieds of the nineteenth century might find it laughable to hear how often they are nowadays depicted as dependent. They were frequently on their knees scrubbing the floors of the wealthy, or staying awake all night to finish sewing a dress for a society lady. They weren't in a position to be referred to as "aggressive" or "strong-willed" as many of today's working women are. Names *were* found for them, however, if they stayed single past marriageable age. "Thornback" was probably one of the worst, referring to a long-time single woman who was assumed to have hardened like a thorny-backed fish because she was without a man.

Today's tough older single women, however, are looked upon with new respect. It's as if younger women realize that it takes something special—in attitude, genetics, luck, lifestyle and inner resources to make it to old age as a single woman and still be in there slugging.

The opportunity to lead an independent and self-sufficient life is reflected in recent trends. Although nearly 90 percent of all adults will eventually marry, they're doing so at a later age, which helps boost statistics on the numbers of adults now living as singles to 37 percent, up from just 28 percent in 1970. In addition to postponement of marriage, there is the divorce rate of nearly 50 percent, coupled with the tendency of divorcees to remain single longer before remarrying. Better job opportunities for women who never marry, and extended life expectancy for widows also add to the growing number of singles.

The Census Bureau projects that by the turn of the century more than 4 million families will be headed by single women ages 45 to 64, compared to about 1 million headed by men of the same age. But the really startling news is that non-family households comprised of singles or those not living with relatives will grow faster than occupied households: 40 percent growth in non-families compared to 37 percent in families.

The climb in the number of single women, though, isn't peculiar to the 1990s. From the late 1800s to the early 1900s there was a movement among women of educated classes to remain single, mostly out of a desire to refrain from an institution they considered stifling. Others feared pregnancy, which was at high risk for complications, and even death, in those days.

The choice to remain single hinged on a woman's ability to support herself or her having inherited wealth, much as it does today. The few notable women of the nineteenth and early twentieth centuries—suffragettes, artists, writers—who made it on their own had sources of income beyond what they could earn.

Nevertheless, the reason so many chose to remain single (up to 11 percent, a ratio never again reached in modern times) remains an enigma. In the early 1900s, nearly 15 percent of the women graduating from prestigious Wellesley College never married, says Janet Giele, a sociologist at Brandeis University.

"People believe this happens because women who are better educated, or at a relatively higher end of the social scale, traditionally tend to marry up or at least on the same level," says Giele. "When there is a scarce pool of men of equal or higher status, the women would rather not marry than marry down. At the beginning of the century, when women first received college educations, there was a great deal of concern that to educate women would end the reproduction of the human race."

By the end of the nineteenth century it was becoming

clear that as the number of single women mounted, so did the demand for access to higher education, a demand that helped create women's colleges. Most state colleges opened their doors to women, although many male educators had doubts that women could make it through higher education without harming themselves mentally and physically.

Kathryn Black, the psychology professor, says that with the recent rapid increase in college-educated women, they too are having trouble finding available mates, men who are as educated, wealthy or energetic as themselves. She believes that the lack of men who have these qualities contributes to the growing numbers of single women. She also believes that if there were enough of these men, women would rather be married than single. "Most women would prefer to be married, but since it isn't an option, they're not going to be unhappy about it," Black says.

Higher education isn't the only obstacle to finding a suitable mate. Historically, women in general have married men a few years older than themselves. Women in this age group outnumber men of the same age. This disparity can be offset by marriage to men in a variety of age groups. A recent trend is for older women to marry younger men.

"I don't think it's a coincidence that many older women are dating younger men," says sociology professor Elizabeth Grauerholz. "I don't know whether they have figured it out yet, but younger men are a different breed. They have grown up with mothers who are working and they have been taught to fend for themselves. They look at women differently. A woman who is independent and taking care of herself can be appealing to them."

Psychologist Marcia Lasswell agrees with Grauerholz.

"There are lots of women dating younger men," she says. "Men who grew up after the sixties have a different viewpoint and attitude than the previous generation."

The National Center for Health Statistics reports that of the annual 2 million marriages 22 percent involve older women and younger men, up from 16 percent in 1970. Nearly 40 percent of brides between the ages of 35 and 44 marry younger men and 45 percent of women over 45 marry younger men.

In 1985 the Census Bureau found that of more than 250,000 women ages 35 to 44, 32 percent were living with younger men, compared to 18 percent five years previously. Of nearly 200,000 women ages 45 to 64, 23 percent were living with younger men. Sociologists say there are benefits to such liaisons since men tend to peak sexually at about 18 and women when they're nearly 40.

Because men of equal educational and socioeconomic levels or in a preferred age group are more difficult to find, some women marry down just as they did in past generations. Women of the late 1800s also married "beneath themselves," which is why literature of the period features the schoolmarm who marries the cowboy or farmer.

In addition to the standard reasons they give for not marrying, women today say they love independence, that they can make it financially without a man, and that singleness doesn't carry the stigma it once did.

Some women who have never married or who are divorced or widowed hold strong feminist views and don't find those views compatible with marriage. Southern historians credit the abolition of slavery with the rise in female singlehood in the South, the reason being that some Southern women realized that they had been little more than chattel themselves.

When men outnumbered women, as they did in certain parts of America prior to the 1900s, it gave those women greater choice in selecting mates.

"There's no single answer, and the answers aren't the same in each historical period," says Giele. "It's an interactive thing for some people. Maybe they don't find anyone who is particularly attractive to them and they develop a self-sufficient way of living. They quit looking. There are others, however, who make it a conscious decision. There is a well-known quote from M. Carey Thomas, the president of Bryn Mawr College at the turn of the century. She said, 'Only our failures marry.'"

History has neglected single women. Although thousands of books and hundreds of films have told the stories of the settling of the West, the role of single women in this effort has been overlooked. Women of the West were depicted as either showgirls or farm wives, despite the fact that some single women homesteaded on their own, joining with men for the best available land.

Because these stories went untold, women who today might otherwise choose to be single don't have maps to follow. We're left with articles and books telling us that women are desperate to get married or remarried, that it's difficult to "make it" alone.

The lack of positive role models leaves society with an ambiguous image of solo women. Are we evil or praiseworthy?

Mostly, we've been considered evil. By the late 1800s, church leaders had become concerned about the increasing numbers of single women. They considered it against God's law for women to forego marriage. Even today, some religious denominations hold that "Women are to be under the umbrella of man who serves as the protector." Although the number of single women continued to increase in the early twentieth century, it dropped dramatically during and after World War II which ushered in the baby boom generation, followed by the baby-bust generation of the 1970s and 1980s. About that time the cycle began again with the beginnings of growth in the number of singles.

"Actually, what we're seeing is a return to a more normal proportion of singles," says Giele. "Prior to World War II, 15 to 20 percent of the population stayed single."

A major difference now is the change in family structure. "We're seeing the phenomenon of single women deciding to have babies," she says.

There is still a stigma attached to single women with babies. "There is a contradiction in our mentality as to whether it's okay to be a single mother," says Giele. "For women who can afford it, such as executives, it's viewed as okay. For poor women and teens it's not okay. We see the latter groups as a burden on society. Clearly, economics plays an important role in the choice to have a child as a single."

This wasn't an issue for earlier generations. If you were single, it was assumed you'd remain celibate. Service to God or some other lofty calling was usually concomitant to your choice, and sexual abstinence was a must. Literature is replete with stories of "fallen" women of the day, or of single women who didn't quite fit the mold. Women today, wrestling with the choice between marriage and singlehood, face similar dilemmas.

In *Liberty, A Better Husband*," Lee Virginia Chambers-Schiller describes a New York woman of the late 1800s who reflects on the many disadvantages of marriage while voicing her fear of becoming an "old maid."

Worries about becoming an old maid might not be a major concern today, but the threat of AIDS may force us to consider celibacy (see chapter 6).

In earlier times, it was religious orders that first opened the educational doors to females, an opportunity that was, for the most part, denied them in the secular world, and which endowed women with a certain amount of autonomy.

By the turn of the century when more and more family units moved from rural settings to urban ones, women gained new freedom of choice. Other single women headed where jobs were available. Ultimately women outnumbered men in the industrial cities. Because of the availability of work, jobs were precarious, and women, then as now, worried about the future—especially about the time when they would no longer be able to work and provide for themselves. These images are undoubtedly similar to present-day fears of becoming "bag ladies."

Then, as now, some impetus to marry was financial. Certainly today's divorced woman with two children and a low-paying job has more need to find a mate than a woman who has a well-paying career or a family inheritance.

In the past, even as women were receiving a message of emancipation, running parallel with this message was the one telling women that marriage was their highest calling.

Chambers-Schiller writes of the warnings to these early independent women: "In maintaining the appearance of hesitation and humility women guarded themselves against charges of ambitiousness. Antebellum literature warned women, and spinsters in particular, against the snare of ambition, the most unfeminine of qualities. This hostility indicated an awareness of women's desire to expand their horizons and to accomplish something of moment."

Those who chose independence faced impoverishment. Losing one's job was tantamount to entering the poorhouse. Most married women didn't have the money to support an impoverished female friend, and the families of these single women often refused to help them unless as spinsters they stayed in the fold and served as caretakers to other family members.

Women of the eighteenth and nineteenth centuries were viewed within the context of their families, and not as independent beings. Even if they chose independence, they were expected to return home when their aging parents needed them or if other members of the family became ill. To refuse to return was to face ostracism.

This still happens today. Stormy Sandquist, a New Mexico artist, said that when her mother, with whom she'd never gotten along, was "killing herself" back in Florida, her mother's friends wrote and told Stormy she should come back and take over. "The idea was that I was single and didn't have a family, so this is what I should do. Whatever my life or career or home situation was had no bearing on the case. My life was insignificant and unimportant. I felt great resentment."

The guilt many of the early singles suffered for choosing a role different from the norm enhanced their need to achieve and prove to themselves and others that they had chosen well. The stress of overreaching, and the discrimination they encountered, caused many to suffer a lifetime of physical illness.

Others who were seemingly stronger were viewed as overly aggressive (does this have a familiar ring?), proud, stubborn and strong-willed.

This situation began to change by the twentieth century when the economy needed single women as workers. What good was a married woman with children to an industrialist? Single women suddenly looked good. An economy that needs women in the work-force makes it easier for women to make it on their own, even if the pay is meager.

We find opportunities for well-paying jobs today. When women are needed in high-paying jobs, society smiles on a woman who will give up home and hearth to move the economy forward. Entrepreneurs are welcome in the business community, and women are in the majority in small-business start-ups.

"It's easier now in our society because more women are going to college," says Kathryn Black. "Society accepts the fact that women have the right and obligation to support themselves. It takes away some of the pressure on you to marry. If someone stays single she has the choice of being happy or miserable. She doesn't have to imagine that a man will make her happier," says Black.

Margaret Adams writes in her book *Single Blessedness* that in England after World War I women found employment opportunities in record numbers while the number of marriages dropped. The war had decimated the pool of available young men.

"The lasting outcome of these massive social changes was that single women became an accepted feature of normal society's fabric and in this role received both respect and support," Adams writes. She adds that the decision to be single has more to do with societal influences and social events than it does with one's own choice.

Black believes that today's society doesn't put as much pressure on women to get married, but that parents and close family members still do. Parents especially will put pressure on daughters to provide grandchildren, and to an older generation, this means marriage for the most part.

For a number of reasons, society doesn't push for a greater birthrate. One reason is that at certain times in history, nations have been unable to support a large growth in population. When this happens, the ruling powers adopt a singles-are-okay attitude. If the trend continues long enough, society eventually adopts laws that benefit singlehood.

It would seem that today's concern with overpopulation would further the cause of singleness, and this may be just what's happening. The number of singles keeps increasing. Laws are not yet keeping up with this trend, but as with most changes in society, laws are the last to follow—usually 20 years later.

Today we still have blatant discrimination against singles and in every area of life—from purchasing membership in health spas (sometimes an entire family can buy membership for the same price as a single) to airline fares where spouses fly free or at half-fare during airline promotions. This discrimination, and what's being done about it, are discussed further in chapter 4.

Literature of the 1800s and early 1900s refers to women like Susan B. Anthony, Sarah Pugh, Sallie Holley, Clara Barton, Emily Blackwell, and hundreds like them, as "hermaphrodite spirits," "man-haters," "lesbians," "deranged," and other obnoxious terms. Many of these women's lives ended in unhappiness. Some were placed in mental institutions. Others took to their beds and died slow deaths. A reading of history clearly shows that their struggles were great, and the odds they confronted and the minimal support they obtained from the general population was so bad that they were literally driven crazy.

Although there are some added burdens placed on single women in American society in the 1990s, they are mild compared to discrimination practiced in other parts of the world.

In *Man Suffocated by Potatoes*, it's said that in Thailand the reruns of the television sitcom "Laverne and Shirley," the adventures of two zany single women, are introduced as a series about two women who have escaped from a lunatic asylum. Single independent women who live apart from their families defy Thai tradition, so that TV executives reasoned that women who choose to be single should be portrayed as crazy.

Women in the U.S. have more choices. Our world isn't exactly an oyster, but it's certainly easier for us to accomplish the things we set out to do than it was for our female ancestors.

Women who choose to be single today may be thought odd, but not negatively so. Minorities are always questioned and scrutinized more carefully than the majority. But as minorities, single women sometimes end up getting more out of life because they have to reach deeper inside and develop themselves more fully just to survive.

If our predecessors hadn't been so frustrated, it's quite possible they wouldn't have driven themselves crazy trying to accomplish what they did. Had they not done so, though, we wouldn't have the vote, access to higher education, or sports scholarships. We live in an atmosphere that makes it easier for us to remain single, thanks to earlier women who paved the way for us. Many of the hang-ups single women have today are thus self-inflicted. Granted, it is difficult not to meet society's expectations that we marry. Looking back, however, it's clear that being single is easier today.

The irony is that the flowering of female singlehood in the eighteenth and nineteenth centuries was viewed with less suspicion than it was later on when Freud and others portrayed female singlehood as unnatural or deviant behavior, and the onus continues intact in the thinking of today's mental health community.

We live in a society that honors the married couple and acts as if those who choose to be single have something wrong with them. The push to marry is so great that at times women act as if there were no other choices.

Finding Mr. Right has a bad name in the 1990s. The search implies the existence of a Prince Charming who will make a woman complete, not to mention happy ever after.

Looking for Mr. Right might not be a bad idea if a woman decides she wants to get married. She can set her standards and then go about an earnest search to find a man. But what she must not do is settle for less than a quality marriage, which is equal to a quality singlehood.

At no time in history have we had such opportunities to live well as singles. True, this option might not be ideal, but then, neither are all marriages.

Future Foibles

Marriage will remain a goal for most men and most women, but the number of singles will continue to increase. In the future there will be more single women with children. The big issues will be the status of children, child care and child support.

Divorce will continue to account for a large proportion of singles, but some experts believe that marriages will improve because more women will have the option of being single.

"They [women] don't have to think that a man will make them happier," says Kathryn Black. "They're happy already and that will lead to stronger marriages. In fact, the divorce rate has already led to stronger marriages in the sense that you don't have to stay in a bad marriage. Obviously, if you don't have to stay in a bad marriage for economic reasons, then you don't have to get married in the first place."

"Put all the current trends together, and what you have is a much larger cohort of adults who are single at any given time," says sociologist Graham B. Spanier of Oregon State University.

Spanier believes that growth in the single population will stimulate the economy. A demand for increased household products will come from smaller households being formed in increasing numbers.

"Social pressure to be married or to be part of a couple has always been strong, but those social pressures are diminishing," says Spanier. "Lifestyles in modern America make it harder to be happily married for an extended period of time."

"It's easier to be single today," he says. "The changing status of women has contributed to this. The educational attainment of women is at an all-time high. Marriage as opposed to a career isn't as compelling as it once was. This is a massive change."

Spanier expects to see a moderate growth in the proportion of people remaining single. Society won't look dramatically different a decade from now, he believes.

"I think women have more alternatives, and getting married isn't viewed as the prized thing it once was," he says. "Women will consider their options. Being widowed or divorced is easier now than it was in 1950, both economically and socially. As a result, more women who have been married will choose to stay single," says Spanier.

Dr. Rege Stewart of the University of Texas Southwestern Medical Center at Dallas believes women are gradually becoming more comfortable with singlehood. A wife of 20 years, Stewart believes the outlook for singles is better than when she married.

"There was a time when men were intimidated by independent women, but that has changed," she says. "This realization came to me at a recent psychiatric meeting. I ran into an old friend whom I hadn't seen for years. We went to dinner together, both on expense accounts. I noticed he was a little distressed and I asked if he would be offended if we asked for separate checks. I could see he was relieved."

Stewart admitted that only a few years ago asking such a question would have been embarrassing for both parties. It was expected that the man would pay for dinner, even if the woman had a professional expense account.

In the past, people married in order to bear legitimate children, to divide labor in a way that was functional, to enjoy socially sanctioned intercourse, and for emotional bonding and attachment, says Theodore Groat, a sociologist at Bowling Green State University.

"When you look at it today, who needs a functional division of labor?" he asks. "No man needs somebody to cook for him or do his laundry. He'll go down to the corner store, use a microwave, and take his shirts to the cleaner. Women don't need the man to bring home the bacon, so to speak, because they're out in the labor force themselves.

"We haven't needed socially sanctioned intercourse since the 1950s," he says. "So there are no compelling reasons to marry. By and large, men and women don't have the same needs to enter into the marital state."

Nevertheless, marriage will still be going strong in the future. It's just that for women who choose to be single, the road will be a little easier and they will find a more accepting society in which to live.

III

The Advantages of Money

Barbara Cunningham has been married several times. She's been single for five years and at the age of 58 finally determined that she's never going to be dependent on a man again. She knows that being on your own requires a certain amount of financial independence.

To this end, after her last divorce from a man who left her with nothing, Cunningham took $9,000 she had inherited from her mother, opened a restaurant and after working 12 to 14 hours daily for four years, sold out with a profit of nearly $200,000.

She took that money and invested it. But she didn't just invest on a whim or turn it over to someone else to manage. Instead she attended school to become an investment counselor. She learned how to take care of her own nest egg and to help other women handle their money wisely. She knows the truth about money now: Money doesn't care who owns it.

Nor does money care how it's spent. It has no mind of its own, so we have to learn how to manage becoming emotionally entangled. Women are newer at the money game than men, and they still have lots to learn. Balancing a checkbook is the easy part. It's learning how to balance money with our lives that's hard.

Jonathan Swift once said, "A wise man should have money in his head, not in his heart."

Ben Franklin said, "The use of money is all the advantage there is in having it."

And Francis Bacon said, "Money is like manure, of very little use except it be spread."

Until recent years, men controlled the financial arena. Some women may have handled the money at home, but it was men who earned it and handed it over.

Elizabeth Cady Stanton, a late nineteenth-century feminist, once said, "Woman will always be dependent until she holds a purse of her own."

The need for income of their own drove some of the early feminists insane. The famous women we read about and admire lived frequently on the verge of poverty. Their lack of money usually was surpassed only by their lack of the means to attain an education. Some went crazy on both fronts. Their great minds were stifled because they worried incessantly about earning a living.

Sound familiar? It should, because we're still doing it. We are still coming out of the Dark Ages when it comes to earning and managing money, even though it's easier for us than it was for our earlier working sisters. Still, say to a room crowded with women that you're concerned about becoming a bag lady in your old age, and heads will turn. I've brought the subject up many times and at least 70 percent of the female listeners will acknowledge they've had similar thoughts, whether married or single, although the single women are more fearful.

Those who didn't become single until they were past the age of 40 are more likely to have visions of a descent in poverty than are younger singles who have grown up in a world where they were encouraged to plan for a career and take care of themselves. However, even the younger women don't discuss finances with the same verve as their male peers.

Before some female Wall Street broker goes for my throat, let me acknowledge that a few women have overcome the financial barrier. But the fact remains, that the majority of women haven't.

It was almost by accident that I took my divorce settlement and bought a small cabin in the mountains. At the time many of my single friends questioned my sanity. "Why don't you travel for a while?" they asked me. "Buy yourself some goodies? Leave your money in the bank?"

But I had fallen in love with this cabin. That's why. And lucky for me. I split the property and built another cabin, which I then rented. That ultimately led to the purchase of another rental, and finally to my overcoming a fear of the stock market.

For someone like myself who has yet to balance her checkbook, this was a miracle. I had to turn for help to the man who sat behind me in the newsroom where I worked as a health reporter. I said to him, "Teach me slowly about investments." He did over a year's time, and I eventually learned how to deal in the stock market.

It didn't come easy. I was raised poor and had never gotten over my fear of poverty.

I've heard people say, "No, no, Rita, you may not have money, but you're not poor. You have talent, love, friends, healthy children. You may not have money, but you have wealth," they told me.

Nonsense. Poor is poor. When I quit my reporter's job to write as a freelance, I once again became "poor" and I'm just now getting my head above water.

It's women's talk that reassures you that if you have

good health, children, friends, et cetera, that you're not poor. Men never say such ridiculous things. They have been trained since infancy to believe that it takes cold hard cash to survive in this country. Ours is a capitalistic society and that's just the way it is. You don't have to sell your soul to the devil for solvency, but women have to get over the idea that money is dirty.

You don't have to be wealthy to be single. But you do have to have the means to provide for yourself. Look around you and take stock of the women who stay in abusive marriages. It's usually because they have small children or don't believe they could support themselves financially.

Elizabeth Grauerholz, a professor of sociology at Purdue University, rates economics as number one in importance for successful single women. "For it [singleness] to be a healthy lifestyle a woman needs economic security," she says. "Women who can choose their living environments have a definite advantage. It's sad, but a lot of women are economically dependent."

Lois Langland, a psychologist and professor at Scripps College in Claremont, California, and who has never married, agrees with Grauerholz. She recalls talking to a young man about women's need to marry for security. She had said that many women aren't looking for the love of their lives, but for the security of their lives. "He looked at me with such horror when I told him some women marry for security," says Langland. "It had never occurred to him."

"Being financially secure helped me to stay on my own," says Audrey Phillips, an 87-year-old one-time real estate agent. "I've always had a good job. During the Depression I made about $750 per month. Even men weren't doing that. Of course, I was working night and day to earn it, but at that time I had the stamina. I worked for the movie studios in wardrobe. I worked all night until 6 A.M., and then they would send us home to eat breakfast. We had to be back by 8 A.M." She married and was widowed at an early age. She credits her early work habits with being able to make it on her own after her husband died.

"You have to be able to feel secure and you don't have to be super-rich to do that," says career counselor De Creasy. "But you have to feel you are able to make your bills every month and have a little set aside and have a place to call your own."

Divorcee Betty Wold draws a small pension and uses her avocations of herbalist, lecturer and writer as a means of earning extra money. It wasn't until she went through her divorce that she learned how important money was, and that her interests had monetary value.

"When I was first divorced, I finally realized that now I was the one who had the job. I paid all the bills. I wanted to open up my own charge account but the company wouldn't let me. I contacted a women's group and they wrote the company and made them give me my own account. I was very insecure after I left my husband. I went into therapy and finally realized that I was a lot better than I had thought I was. I finally sued my ex. After the divorce I felt he should pay some support. He tried to bully me out of it."

His threats didn't work and Wold says it was a turning point for her because she found out, through the need for money, that she was of value and always had been.

Glenna McAnish offers a different perspective: "I used to tell people that I've been so hard up I could give poor lessons. You have to learn to feel *broke*, not poor. You have to be tricky to get by. It's called survival. If you don't have the spirit for it, you'll just end up getting married again."

With few exceptions, women are seldom taken seriously when it comes to money. Some complain that men won't discuss money matters with them the way they will with other men. Single women report that when they are talking with a man, and another man enters the conversation, the subject matter changes to heavier topics such as investments and banking.

One morning while eating breakfast in a restaurant I picked up a copy of the *Wall Street Journal*. The man sitting in the next booth looked over at me and said, "You don't see too many women reading the *Journal*."

And consider the following true story told me by a single woman in her early 50s who owns her own publishing company. She's not only business smart, but she's gorgeous as well, and talks with a lilting Texas accent. While at a bookseller's convention she met a man, another publisher, who asked her out to dinner. She was intrigued because he seemed cosmopolitan, accepting of professional women and enlightened. And he was handsome. As the evening progressed she found herself thinking, "Hey, this guy's not so bad. I could see myself having a relationship with him."

A few seconds after that thought went through her mind, he grabbed her hand across the table, and while holding it and looking into her eyes he said, "Come on. Tell me what sugar daddy is really financing your company."

The blame for this man's stupid question doesn't lie entirely with him. Much of it has to do with his own observations about women and money. Women have to accept some of the responsibility.

"Our sense of personal worth is wrapped up in notions of relationships, nurturing and caregiving," says Mara Adelman. "Those are important qualities, but we resist quantifying ourselves in monetary terms.

"You really can't talk about developing strong support systems until you recognize the link to the financial," she adds. "It's said that money can't buy friends, but my response to that is to say 'baloney.'

"When someone invites you out to dinner, you're not independent if you don't have the money to reciprocate. If you can't reciprocate you're in an indentured and indebted relationship. Money represents choices. It opens up options for a woman. It helps women control their environments."

"Granted, women don't have good role models when it comes to finances. But I think it goes deeper. It's the way we see ourselves. We have a hell of a time negotiating money. Women in the know say this is the bane of our existence," says Adelman.

We're a capitalistic society, and nearly everything from the school system to the type of makeup a woman wears has something to do with the economy. So it makes sense to learn the rudiments of money management.

There are at least five beginning steps to managing money. The first was taught to me by the same financial editor who enlightened me about stocks.

(1) *Learn the language of money.* Once you master the language of any discipline you have begun to understand that discipline. Then you incorporate it into your life.

In order to understand, say, a computer, you read about

it. You ask others about it. You share with others. You take classes in it. It may seem boring at first. Eventually it's kind of fun to hold your own in a conversation about finances—or computers, for that matter.

When I began my education in money matters, I started watching Luis Rukeyser on public television every Friday night. At first I asked myself, "Why should I watch something so boring? This program speaks only to people who already have money, and it's so cold and impersonal."

Well, after watching it a while, I determined that Rukeyser was cute, that I was picking up some tips on the language of money, and that there were women on his show who ran investment firms.

(2) *Let your money work for you.* You don't have to be a hard-nosed bitch to be interested in investing money. One of my former editors, a vibrant redhead who loved to shop at Nordstrom, was given a birthday present of a stock in that company by her husband. He told her, "Now maybe you'll get some of your money back." This is called letting your money work for you. As one famous television commercial put it, "It isn't how much you earn, but how much you save that counts." This editor made a lot of sound investments on her own, lest you label her an "airhead."

Another way of looking at investing, especially if you're on a budget, is: Instead of buying that gorgeous new outfit, invest the same amount of money in the company that manufactured it.

If you're serious about investments, you may want to contact a financial planner or other financial advisor. In her book *Terry Savage Talks Money*, the award-winning financial journalist warns consumers that anyone, from real-estate salespeople to insurance agents, can call themselves "financial planners" simply by hanging out their shingles. For referrals to qualified planners, she recommends contacting the International Association for Financial Planning at 2 Concourse Parkway, Suite 800, Atlanta, Georgia, 30328; the College of Financial Planning in Denver, Colorado, at (303) 220-1200; or the American College (which grants the degree of chartered financial consultant) at 270 Bryn Mawr Ave., Bryn Mawr, Pennsylvania, 19010.

(3) *Establish a system to pay your bills.* It took me 10 years to realize that I didn't have to pay a bill the minute it appeared in my mailbox. Look at the due dates on your bills and pay them two days before it's due, or however long you figure it will take to get to the company by mail on time. That way, your money works for you—in the bank right up until the moment it's due. Why pay something 30 days in advance when that money could be earning you money?

To this end, I now write the date to pay a certain bill on the envelope in which it arrives.

(4) *Design some sort of budget.* Actually, a budget can work to your advantage not only by acting as a guide to bill-paying, but it will sometimes also force you to spend more money on yourself.

When I went into freelance writing, I quit spending money on pleasure because I was fearful of the bag-lady syndrome. Eventually, I was forced to realize that all work and no play really does make for a dull person. My writing lagged because I wasn't letting go once in a while. A budget not only reminds you that you have commitments to meet, but that you also have a soul that needs attending to. Budgets pay bills *and* buy flowers.

(5) *Avoid irrational spending.* Think things through before you part with your money, and don't charge what you can't pay off that same month.

I've known women to charge entire vacations and then have to work an entire year to pay it off. A good look at the psychology of this will tell you that the trip will be much more enjoyable if you pay as you go. Resentment can build up if you're always paying for things in the wake you leave. It's like being the last wagon in a wagon train going over a dusty mountain pass. It can leave a gritty taste in the mouth.

Another suggestion for getting over the budget hurdle is to take some basic courses in money management.

There is, however, always the possibility that adverse conditions could cause a major setback in your finances. Therefore one source of income shouldn't be overlooked if the need ever arises: the available social services, regardless of what you imagine others will think.

As Americans, we're entitled to these services. As workers, former workers, former wives, and mothers we have every right to draw from these sources. There is never a need to feel guilty about asking for help. And there is no need to feel ashamed when applying for any of these services, even welfare, although the process is cold and unsympathetic. When I was applying for Medi-Cal (California's version of Medicaid) for my mother, who has Alzheimer's, I dreaded talking to the social workers because they had such bad attitudes. The worker who was handling my mother's case, for example, asked me to refer to her (the caseworker) by such-and-such number when I called. How sad that what should be a proud and distinguished helping profession has become so impersonal.

For those of you who might harbor a grudge against our welfare system, who believe the extreme conservatives in our society who perpetuate the myth that welfare recipients are cheats, let's look at the reality—the average welfare recipient is a 24-year-old white woman with two children who is usually in the system for approximately nine months. Only 5 percent of those on welfare are what could be called "cheats." They make all the rest look bad. Welfare is there for those in need.

That the system needs reform is true. It needs more job training, education and self-esteem builders for chronic recipients of welfare. As women, we should be the first to remember that many of those on welfare are women who have no other choice. And the majority of them are single.

Sociologist Barbara Cambridge says that when she's working with single mothers who feel guilty about receiving subsidies, she tells them to lighten up. "Society may look down on them, but I tell them not to let anyone put that burden on them," she says. "We talk about being single and what they can do with that singleness. I remind them that when their food stamps run out before the end of the month, they have learned to network to make it.

"The fact that they feel responsible for their children, and that they use creative ways to make it the best they can for their families, shows their strengths," she says.

Cambridge acknowledges that the financial burdens faced by low-income, poorly educated women make them vulnerable to degrading relationships. But even women who have good jobs and educations have trouble dealing with the financial facets of their lives, and Cambridge believes they can learn from her welfare mothers.

"I begin by asking them to take a look at themselves, to visualize an image of themselves and then to project that image into five years from now. How do they see themselves then? What is the self-perception that they carry around now, and what is the one they would like to have? If there is a negative perception, I work with them on changing that because as long as it's negative, that's what they will be," she says.

Just the opposite is the woman who has a high image of herself and who loves her work. But she too can be vulnerable. It's okay for men to fall in love with their work, visions, inventions and the arts, but women are on shakier ground. "We've approved it for men. It's a romantic and popular image for them, but it hasn't yet been approved for women," says communications professor Mara Adelman, who acknowledges that when she is on a roll in her own work, months can go by when she doesn't think about men or relationships.

"Men find that very threatening," she says. Women find it threatening too, even those who support themselves. We erroneously feel that it's somehow "not right to feel this good about our work."

Another area in which we can take lessons from men is in retirement planning. Men seem to be much more aware that some day they are going to retire and that it takes more than a gold watch to keep above the poverty level.

This danger was illustrated for me by a friend, a technotwit who programmed my future financial picture based on my savings, earning capacity and social security retirement into a computer. The picture was one of gloom, and until then I had refused to look at it realistically.

I had, however, protected my children by establishing

a will and a living will. The will is simple and splits all my assets equally among my children in the event of my death. The will stipulates that if I become incapacitated, they are to be given power of attorney to make personal and financial decisions for me. The living will stipulates that I'm to be given no extraordinary life-saving measures in the event of catastrophic disease or accident.

I'm in the process of upgrading the will and living will, however. The simple will may not be enough to completely carry out my wishes, especially if I become incapacitated, and the living will is more a directive to physicians which is not honored in all states.

In place of the living will, a durable power of attorney for health care is needed. It designates a particular person or persons to make health care decisions for you if you are unable to do so. It gives designated people the authority to tell a physician or hospital staff to "pull the plug." Many state medical associations provide forms that grant durable power of attorney for health care, as do some stationery stores.

A living trust, revocable or irrevocable, is drawn up by an attorney. It saves family members from having to go through probate. In a living trust, all property and assets are placed in trust with instructions on how they are to be distributed upon death. The revocable trust allows the person to change the conditions of the trust at any time.

I've seen a variety of living trusts drawn up by different attorneys. Some are good documents and some are awful. In order to have one drawn up properly, I would suggest contacting your local bar association and asking for a specialist. Or, consider one who is referred by a friend.

All of these issues, from earning money and investing it, to planning for retirement and for death, fall under the category of "finances."

Finances are an emotional issue. They have made and ruined empires. Is it any wonder we approach our personal finances with trepidation?

IV

Street Smarts, or Down with Discrimination

What Discrimination?

As women, we know the face of discrimination. Collectively and individually, we try to remedy the situation. But singles also receive their share of discrimination, so as single women we get a double whammy.

Anyone who followed the nomination of Supreme Court Justice David Souther has seen the bias against singles. Here's an m-a-n whose credibility was questioned solely because he was a bachelor.

Ralph Nader too has been questioned about his single status. In fact, when a man reaches 40 and has never married, many people presume he's gay, asexual or just plain odd.

Consider a chilling fundamentalist Christian outlook on singles as reported in a March 29, 1990, article in the *Los Angeles Times*: Beverly Sheldon, whose husband, the Reverend Louis P. Sheldon, heads the Traditional Values Coalition in Irvine, California, was quoted as saying, "Single people aren't providing the same stability to our country, they're not providing offspring, they carry more diseases."

When you can say, "I'm perfectly happy with my life as a single person," you are not making a simple statement. You are among the ranks of a minority population, and you must share some of their burden.

Women used to be considered old maids if they reached their mid-twenties without tying the knot. Now they're questioned about the possibility of their being lesbian. Several women have told me that when they turn down a man's sexual offer, they're sometimes asked outright if they're homosexual, as if that could be the only reason for their refusal. Then there are statements such as, "I can't believe someone like you was never able to get a man."

A particularly bad time for single women is the period immediately after a divorce, when they're considered fair game for every male on the block. Women who have been single long enough believe the high statistics on infidelity among married men. They've had these guys howling around their back porches in the mistaken belief that once-married women "can't live without it." Betty Wold remembers the scene after her divorce: "You would have thought I was in heat. All the dogs of the neighborhood were at my back door."

So far we've dealt with emotional aspects of being single, but there are others to consider. The report from the Consumer Task Force on Marital Status Discrimination, released in 1990 by Los Angeles City Attorney James K. Hahn, found discrimination against local singles in housing, insurance, credit, airlines, membership organizations, hospitals and nursing homes, the funeral industry, newspapers and jails. If this level of discrimination was found in Los Angeles, the singles' capital of the nation, imagine what it is in other parts of the country.

Thomas F. Coleman, law professor at the University of

Southern California Law Center, headed the task force. He says that single women don't yet comprehend how much they're discriminated against in our society. And he adds that because they haven't organized as other minority groups have, they lack power.

Coleman believes that the gay community has taken the lead in demanding equal rights for singles. These demands, backed by years of experience in fighting discrimination and obtaining political clout, will ultimately help other minority groups, such as women who choose to be single.

As examples of overt discrimination against singles, consider the following:

—Airlines that offer cut rates to the "spouses" of frequent flyers.

—Spas and gyms that charge the same dues for a family as for a single person.

—Insurance companies that charge more for singles (or even turn them down) claiming that marital status has a bearing on risk.

—Insurance companies that make it tough for single people to name someone other than a family member as beneficiary to a life-insurance policy.

—Travel clubs that offer discounts to married couples.

—Landlord discrimination against single women, especially if they have children.

—Membership organizations that charge higher dues or fees for singles.

These are only a few examples of discrimination based on single status, but these examples hit singles hard in the pocketbook. The discounts to families and married couples are subsidized by singles.

Dana Brookins remembers a trip to Rhode Island for a

conference in 1989. "I paid $95 for me alone for the same size hotel room a couple occupied. They paid $105. For $10 more they were given the use of two beds, they used two sets of towels, et cetera. There is a big break for couples."

Betty Wold travels quite a bit and she resents the singles' fee tacked on tours. "Sometimes you can bunk with a total stranger, but why don't they have more rooms just for one person?" she asks. (Some hotel chains are beginning to offer special accommodations to singles. See chapter 9.)

Wold also resents the family-size packaging that is cheaper in the supermarkets. She gets ticked at things like bank promotions that provide two dinners for the price of one. She believes it's a subtle reminder that banks trust families more than singles.

Some changes are being made, however. Law professor Thomas Coleman notes that the Greater Los Angeles Zoo Association now offers memberships at reduced rates for any two adults, regardless of marital status. He explains that some states have enacted laws to protect singles. For example, it's illegal in some states for landlords to refuse to rent to single tenants or for insurance companies to levy higher premiums or refuse insurance coverage to singles.

California has been a leader in developing laws that protect singles in the marketplace, Coleman says. But a few other states are following suit, including New York. For information on your legal rights as a single, start by contacting your state's consumer protection agency or board.

If laws don't exist to protect you in specific areas of concern as a single, sometimes a personal campaign will help, such as writing a letter to an offending agency or business and letting them know how you feel about being discriminated against.

"The law is a codification of society's attitudes," says Coleman. "Social attitudes change but the laws stay on the books until somebody takes up the cause. We've seen changes in sex discrimination because women banded together politically. We've seen changes in terms of gays and lesbians because the gay community banded together politically. But we haven't seen change for singles because they haven't banded together. Singles are still in isolated categories. We have widows, young singles who haven't yet married, unmarried couples, divorced women . . . and none of these groups has individual clout. But when you add them all up, you find nearly 40 percent of the population single at any given time," Coleman says.

The marketplace is starting to pay attention simply because the number of singles is growing. This growth includes an increase in never-marrieds, although nearly 90 percent of the population will eventually marry. The increase in the number of singles is also attributed to the later age at which people are marrying, to divorced people who never remarry, and to widows who choose not to remarry.

By the turn of the century it's expected that 46 percent of the 25-to-44 age group will be single at some time. Being single might be more comfortable in the future, but for now we're affected by discrimination.

Coleman points out that according to laws still on the books in many states, single women can be thrown in jail if a man spends the night with them. Other laws still detail how married couples should go about their sexual activity. States which prohibit sex between unmarried partners of the opposite sex, even if they use the missionary position, include Idaho, Massachusetts, Utah, Arizona, Florida, Louisiana, Mississippi, Alabama, North Carolina,

South Carolina, Georgia, Virginia, Kentucky, Tennessee, Maryland, Oklahoma, Rhode Island, Minnesota, New Mexico and Michigan.

These laws are mostly overlooked. On the other hand, they can be upheld vigorously. The situation is like speeding tickets: they're usually doled out to those who happen to be in the wrong place at the wrong time, by a cop who's had a bad day.

According to Coleman, the laws are most frequently invoked in child custody cases. There was such a case in Rhode Island in 1989 that went all the way to the U.S. Supreme Court. Although the case was summarily rejected by the federal court, the Rhode Island Supreme Court had ruled that the woman was having her boyfriend over periodically, and it granted custody to the father. A similar case was overthrown eventually in Illinois.

In Wisconsin, a 28-year-old woman was ordered to perform 40 hours of community service and attend two months of parental counseling sessions in lieu of charges based on a seldom-enforced adultery law. The woman had pleaded innocent to the adultery charge, but had admitted during a divorce hearing that she had had an extramarital affair in 1989. Her former husband had also admitted to an affair, but he wasn't prosecuted.

Discrimination and Women's Health

Another very serious effect of discrimination against women in general is on health studies. Some of these studies, such as the mental health of single women, are distorted.

Nearly all drug testing involves men only. According to a 1990 report released by the General Accounting Office, which funds all federal medical research, women are usually excluded from other medical research. For example, researchers are just beginning to explore some of the differences between men and women with heart disease (see more on heart disease and women in chapter 8).

In response to this discrepancy, a new advocacy group, called the Society for the Advancement of Women's Health Research, has been formed, and the National Institutes of Health have recently created an Office of Women's Health Research, to include women and minorities in study populations. The new office, which will monitor and coordinate all NIH activities regarding women's health, is headed by Ruth Kirchstein, M.D., director of the National Institute of Medical Sciences.

Shortly after the GAO report was released I received notice from the University of Texas Southwestern Medical Center at Dallas that said: "In the wake of recent Congressional accusations that medical research favors men's health concerns over women's, a researcher at the UTSMCD is embarking on a study that focuses exclusively on post-menopausal women and the most effective means of lowering their blood cholesterol levels." It's almost assured now that studies using women will become routine at research centers.

Unfortunately, much damage has already been done. Because women have been left out of health studies, a network of bias has evolved. One common perception is that being single leads to depression, loneliness and physical illness because the support of a caring partner is missing.

A recent study at the University of Michigan was

reported in newspapers throughout the country with headlines saying that singles suffer "Grave Consequences," that being single is "Dangerous to Your Health," and so on.

Knowing that this information contradicts other new research, I obtained a copy of the study and interviewed one of the researchers, Karl Landis. He agreed that his study never said that being single was bad for your health. What it did say was that marriage was one way to have a social relationship. The article emphasized that social support and social relationships (not necessarily marriage) boost physical and mental health and may add a few years to a person's life.

Landis explained that the animal studies alluded to in the report didn't refer to marriage, but rather to animals living together in groups. "If you look at the study, the index used centered on the frequency of contact with family, friends, neighbors and coworkers," he said.

Other studies have shown that the health benefits of being married are relevant more for men than for women and that becoming widowed is more detrimental for men than for women.

Throughout the 1980s other researchers began reporting that social supports are better predictors of life satisfaction than marital status.

In my interview with a sociologist at a Midwestern university, he insisted that studies still show that unmarried women of marriageable age aren't satisfied with their lives and that they don't rank high on the well-being scale.

When I questioned his viewpoint he relented a little and said, "Well, maybe you're talking to older women. I explained to him that some of the "older" women I was talking to were in their 30s.

"Don't forget," he said, "that many of those older women are widows or women whose husbands have left them for younger women. They've probably rationalized their way into thinking they're happier single. It's human nature to do that."

I countered with my own experience. I had become single at age 39 by choice, had several opportunities to remarry, but had decided that marriage wasn't what I ever wanted again. I had loved my former husband deeply for most of our marriage and have three wonderful kids from that life. I told the sociologist that many women of all ages feel the same way, and I reminded him that many older women are marrying younger men.

I reminded him of newer research showing that single women with satisfying careers rank higher on the well-being scale than married women with or without careers. Those same studies show that it's married men, not married women, who rank far higher on the well-being scale than their unmarried counterparts.

There was a long silence and then he said, "Well, maybe there is something to what you're saying. I've just gone through my second divorce. My ex bought a house right down the street from me and we're still good friends. She said she simply doesn't want to be married." He acknowledged that he doesn't like living alone and plans to remarry as soon as possible.

Men have a tougher time living alone than do women who have some sort of financial independence. Several feminist leaders have maintained that marriage was good for men but not for women.

Another bias is found in the avalanche of books telling women how to find men. They perpetuate the myth that single is somehow synonymous with sad. These books tell women how/where/why/on/and/on they can snag a man, as if that were the major goal in a woman's life.

Granted, at certain ages an important goal for a majority of women *is* to get married and have a family. There is nothing wrong with this. But making women feel desperate does them no service.

An article in a woman's magazine goes so far as to tell women that a good place to meet men (since they're allegedly so hard to find) is at an Alcoholics Anonymous meeting. The men there were considered "safe" because they were recovering alcoholics instead of drunks. If a woman followed that advice, perhaps her next purchase should be a book telling her how not to be a codependent. The author of this bad advice is obviously assuming that women are desperate.

Biases persist even into old age, however. A hefty one is found in the image of the aging single woman. Contrary to popular belief the healthy status of single women doesn't diminish with age. Studies by Marilyn Essex of the University of Wisconsin found that not only is it a myth that women between the ages of 50 and 95 are unhappy or depressed because of the aging process, but that those in that age group who are single are even less unhappy or depressed than their married counterparts.

"The stereotype of their being lonely little old ladies is a myth," says Essex. "We also found that those who had never married were more resilient than those who were formerly married. What we believe is that they were tough to begin with because they chose to be single. A lot of it has to do with having the ability to make this choice. Having a choice is important to one's well-being.

"Also I think it has to do with what you run up against

in life. For instance, we found the formerly married or widowed were more bothered by interpersonal relationships, problems with stress in relationships, and dealing with losses from death.

"The never-married women weren't bothered by that. On the other hand, health problems bothered single women more because the problems were a threat to the independence the women had cherished all their lives."

Essex says that self-reliance is a big issue with single women. They perceive themselves as survivors. As they get older, if they manage to stay self-reliant and independent, they get psychological benefit comparing themselves to aging friends who need more help.

"As they become older and older and are still on their own, they view themselves as special," she says. "By the time you're 85 and still living on your own, you know you are pretty special."

Audrey Phillips, whose second husband died when she was 38, said she came close to marrying three or four times after he died, but always balked because she didn't want to give up her freedom and independence. She had a good job and didn't need the financial security some men give women.

While the stage has been set for a new type of woman who is comfortable as a single, and for a society that accepts singles with open arms, the reality isn't quite here yet.

"Help for singles will come slowly and only when they demand equal rights," says Thomas Coleman. "Companies change when people speak up and write and protest. It won't be until singles view themselves as an oppressed minority that they will take action."

Living in the Here and Now

In the meantime, the best places to live as a single are big cities like Los Angeles, Seattle, New York. Their populations are so diverse that singles can readily find networks of other single friends.

Also, cities with major university communities are more accepting of singles. There are two reasons for this: (1) university communities themselves tend to be more enlightened and integrated, and (2) college campuses draw many single women as instructors.

Lois Langland, a professor of psychology, and who has never married, says that she's always been accepted as a single person in a university town. Much of her social life has centered on university activities, and she's attended functions with the husbands of her coworkers when they had other obligations. In some cases she has been integrated into their families.

Prior to the feminist movement, universities were places for career women to find acceptance. Not that universities haven't been hotbeds of sexual discrimination at times, but they have also been slightly more tolerant.

The best way to feel integrated into the total community, however, is to not limit yourself to single friends only. Langland acknowledges that she treats herself as a family, and likes homemaking and cooking. She recognizes singles are discriminated against, but doesn't let it interfere with her life.

Newspaper editor Elizabeth Bacon has friends of all sorts, married, divorced, widowed and solo. She says she knows a single woman, an attorney for the IRS, who is "obsessed with couples and families. She is a remarkably unattractive woman with a terrible personality who is always saying she wasn't invited to a certain place because she's single." The woman isn't invited anywhere, according to Bacon, not because she's single, but because of her irritable attitude.

We can blame some things on being single—higher tax rates, fewer discounts—and these are things we can fight, but attitude is up to us. If we're comfortable with our singleness, others are more likely to be comfortable with us.

Successful singles share some things in common. They:
—aren't afraid of being seen as a fool.
—have a good sense of humor.
—understand the human condition.
—don't mind standing alone on an issue.
—aren't afraid of being alone.
—respect friendships.
—don't mind breaking taboos.
—will often break tradition.
—can tolerate criticism.
—know that mistakes often lead to success.
—are resilient.

V

How to Be a Bitch and Other Self-Esteem Boosters

The five-mile walk I take around the lake near my house each morning is one of the perks of living as I do—with greater freedom, but little money as a free-lance writer.

Over the course of my walks, certain other walkers, joggers and bicycle riders become familiar. One chilly morning I chatted with a man I'd seen several times on the trail.

The subject of this book came up and before I could see it coming, his voice had risen perceptibly and he said, "I don't believe that. I don't believe there are women who choose not to get married if they have the chance."

"Sorry," I said. "Research is showing differently. There are growing numbers of women choosing to be single."

I threw out a few statistics and qualified the statement by saying that many of these women still have relationships with men, but they choose not to marry.

"Oh, but they live with men, huh?" he said.

"No, they might have relationships, but they choose to live on their own."

"But that goes against what's normal," he said.

I asked him who established what's normal.

After that the conversation deteriorated but his parting

words were, "Boy, I want to read that book when it comes out."

I hope he does, but doubt it will do him much good.

Any woman who's been on her own for some time has been asked why she's not married. Sometimes the question is asked innocently and sometimes it's rhetorical. People ask it as if looking for an opportunity to disagree with the answer. Some will say, "Gee, why are you living by yourself" and they'll wait for a logical answer with a pleasant look on their face. Others might ask, "Why are you single?" with that glint in their eye that shows them to be thinking, "No one would have you." When you answer some with complete honesty, they'll say, "I don't believe you. Every woman wants to get married."

Sorry folks. That last statement's not true. More and more women don't want to get married or remarried. Generally, it's men who want to marry, and they do so rapidly. Most men marry within three years after a divorce, with the greater portion of them doing it within a year. What they then do is carry the same tired, psychological baggage that helped break up the second and the third marriage.

I spoke recently with a male friend who has been separated for about six months and is now going through a divorce. He was considering moving in with a woman he'd known for only a short time. I asked him if he'd thought about taking some time to sort out the problems in his first marriage and spending some time alone so he could grow and get to know himself. He replied, "But what if I meet Miss Right and pass her up? The same opportunity may not come along again."

I nearly fainted. Isn't it supposed to be the stereotypical single woman who is stuck looking for *Mr.* Right?

Widowers, too, are notorious for the urge to remarry. As a newspaper reporter, I once covered a grief support group for widowers and widows. They had a lengthy and serious discussion about loneliness. One woman lightened up the meeting when she described her own experience: "Widowers don't stay that way very long. I live in a mobile-home park and when a wife dies all the widows in the park start bringing over casseroles for the widower. After about a month, he picks the best casserole and he's never lonely again."

Then there was the funeral of a former neighbor which I attended not too long ago. I was among old friends with whom I'd kept in contact; it was the husband of one of them who had died. Sitting around the table later with my friends—all of whom were in some sort of married state, either long-term or second marriage—I was asked why I had never remarried. Before I could reply, another long-married woman replied, "Why the hell do you think she never remarried? Look at us. We were just sitting here bitching about having to get home and do this and do that. She has a choice of what she wants to do when she gets home."

I'm not knocking marriage. It has its own rewards, just as being single does. I'm only saying that it's okay to have a choice, that life doesn't stand still when you're single. Singleness is just another way of spending your time on the planet. There no longer seems to be a need to propagate the earth; we have more than enough people already. Not that we should stop having children. I've had three of my own and "multiplied." It's simply a choice.

Still, we all know uninformed people who ask their married friends, "Why haven't you had children yet?" The same type of person will ask why you're not married.

Rudeness is one of the things you might have to put up with as a healthy single person. Another is being called a bitch. Singles (at least those over what is considered marriageable age) have been depicted for too long as unhealthy, unhappy, lonely, *ad nauseam*, and it just ain't so. But depict us as bitches, and that's okay. Bitchiness is human and sometimes life-preserving.

I'm certain the man I encountered on my walk around the lake has labeled me a bitch. So what?

If we're single we're better off with a little bit of the bitch in us. It helps us take care of chores usually split between men and women—from finances to washing windows to overseeing room additions. Getting some of these jobs done means leaving coyness behind.

If we're healthy singles, we've learned along the way, usually through trial and error, that being good girls won't get us through life, and that trying to please others all the time only makes basket cases out of us.

Another lesson that's difficult to grasp, is that the big bird of paradise flies overhead, dumping on men and women alike. At times we harbor the illusion that because we're women on our own, car mechanics, construction contractors and investment consultants are all out to do us in.

What we fail to understand is that men get taken just as readily as women. I know men who can't find the dipstick in their own cars. I know men who are awful with their finances. And do men really get treated better when they're having a house remodeled? Not at all, some of the worst such horror stories have come from the mouths of men.

If we're going to be single by choice, we've got to stop whining and start bitching.

In retrospect, some of the things that make us bitch turn out to be funny. They're the fodder of rich lives. For example, when I was having a house built, I encountered some of the worst sexism I've ever dealt with.

I had made it a point to become familiar with every phase of the construction, and each evening when I returned home from work, I did an inspection tour. This particular day the plumber was working beneath the house, which had a five-foot foundation because it was built on a flood plain. I crawled underneath with him and began asking questions about which pipes led where and took care of what.

Once outside again, my lazy-looking dog, Annie, ambled over. The plumber scratched Annie behind her ear and then said, "Why can't you just be nice and gentle and easy-going like your dog?"

I found his remark too stupid to answer. Instead I started laughing and didn't quit until he hopped into his truck and drove off.

He probably considered me a bitch because I was nosing beneath my house into what he considered his business. My laughing and refusing to reply to his remark probably added to his impression of my bitchiness. If we raise our voices we will surely be called a bitch. Most of us know the cliché that a man can be considered assertive, and that under the same circumstances a woman's response is considered bitchy. The fact is that whatever gets the job done is what's needed. Some situations lend themselves to bitchiness. Sometimes we get tired of explaining why we're single and we are downright surly about it.

Newspaper editor Elizabeth Bacon was once approached by a husband and wife at her church and asked to head a committee. They phrased their request like this: "We thought you might have more time than we do since you're single."

She explained to them that her time was probably *more* limited because she took care of jobs that were usually split between two people. Mundane chores such as shopping, cooking, cleaning, house repairs, yard work, paying bills, and maintenance of the car were all hers. Perhaps the couple was thinking what a bitch she was as they turned away.

Bacon knows she could hire someone to take care of some of her chores, but she says, "Oakies like me don't hire things done." The real reason single women do so much of their own work is that finding responsible people to do it for them is difficult. I once referred a contractor to a friend. He had made some minor repairs without problems at my cabin, but he arrived at my friend's disguised as Mr. Destructo. She finally paid him some money when he promised *not* to come back and finish the job.

Betty Wold, the Oklahoma herbalist and author of *Speaking of Herbs*, says she could solve the problem with a brother-in-law book. She's had to hire a few things done around her country home, like mending broken water pipes and repairing electrical breakdowns. When she found someone reliable to fix, say, the plumbing, she'd ask if they also did electrical work. They'd always answer, "Noooo, but I've got a brother-in-law who does that."

"I would just sit back and wait a week or two and, sure enough, a brother-in-law would show up for the other job," she says.

Barbara Cambridge, the Texas sociologist, says she has plenty of friends or neighbors to call on, and her son volunteers to do stuff, "but I wouldn't let any of them do chores for me. I've developed a list over the years of people I can hire. I don't use my male neighbors, friends or relatives to do this work for me. They have their own families. If I needed help in an emergency, though, I would ask and they would come."

Most of us who choose to be single don't rely on others to do chores for us on a regular basis. But like most of humanity, we have been helped by friends and family on occasion, and when we need help we welcome it.

When people volunteer their time to help you, though, you don't have the right to bitch. My grown children have helped me move several times during the 14 years I've been single. At one time I owned three cabins and found myself moving back and forth between them as I fixed them up. I owned a gigantic refrigerator that took creative ability to get in and out of the cabins. After the fifth move, my son Dawson put his foot down. "Okay. I'll help you move anytime," he promised, "but never again will I move the refrigerator." I took him seriously and traded off the refrigerator before the next time I moved. I plan to stay where I am now, and my children have all breathed a sigh of relief.

Paul Hilsdale, a Los Angeles psychotherapist, asked me rhetorically one time, "What's wrong with being a bitch?" He pointed out that Kali, the Hindu cannibal-mother goddess, is the personification of a bitch, both life-giver and life-destroyer, and yet she's worshipped.

You're Not Getting Older, You're Getting Bitchier

Another bit of folderol we've heard all our lives is that it isn't how old you are but how young you feel. That's the same as telling a poor person she's not poor (see chapter 3). Telling someone that age doesn't matter is just a euphemism to make the person avoid facing reality. I happen to believe it's easier to fight the enemy when you can see what it looks like.

Every woman can treat aging just as she wishes. Ever since one of my friends turned 50, she has insisted that she be given a senior's discount wherever possible—to the point of arguing with a clerk in public. Another acquaintance, also married, who just turned 70 and has the figure of a 30-year-old along with a youthful face, would protest being called a senior citizen even if it meant turning down a free month-long trip to Europe.

Single women friends are no different. Some flaunt their age like a badge of honor and others stay mum on the subject. Katharine Hepburn was once complimented for aging gracefully and retorted that it really wasn't fun to look in the mirror every day and witness your own dying process. We're all entitled to handle our aging processes in our own way.

Samuel Coleridge, the eighteenth-century poet and critic, said, "There are three classes into which all the women past seventy years of age I have ever known were divided: that dear old soul; that old woman; that old witch."

I like to think that when I'm 70, I'll be a combination of all three.

Being a bitch with no apologies means accepting both our good and bad sides. A gentle and fierce disposition. A submissive and bold character. A bitchy and a loving personality.

They Should Have Bitched Instead

As-told-to stories:

When I was visiting a friend, Nancy Hardy, at her home on the outskirts of Chicago we were making plans to go see a play at one of the theaters. Hardy called another friend who lived in downtown Chicago to see if she wanted to join us. Her friend said she couldn't because she was kind of broke, and had decided to spend her limited resources going only to places where she could meet men.

There was this really nice single woman in Newback, Oklahoma. She'd been widowed about 15 years. She was fun, witty and interesting. I liked her real well, but she was desperate to get married again. Just desperate.

Anytime a single man showed up on the horizon, she was out to get him. She would invite him to dinner. Make these wonderful meals. She made no bones about the fact that she wanted to get married again. I don't think she ever stopped to look at how happy she was as a single woman. So anyhow, this man moved nearby and his wife had just died about six months before, and some of these men are too lazy to do something for themselves. They look for a new wife to do it. She married him and he promptly developed crippling arthritis. She has had to wait on him all the time. He did have money to buy her a beautiful house but she's at his beck and call. Now her health is failing too from taking care of him.

I think she could have been very happy as a single if she had only stopped and looked at how nice her life was then.

Where I worked there were a couple of sexual harassment cases, so management met with people from all departments to discuss the issue. There was this guy from circulation who was real irritated at having to attend the meeting. "I don't see any reason to be here," he complained. "I treat all the girls in my office just fine."

I asked him how old his "girls" were.

He said, "Don't talk to me like that."

Somebody told me about these two women who were going someplace and they invited a third and she really wanted to go, but she wouldn't because she believed that men would approach two women but not three.

A widow tells the following story. "Financially it was very bad when he was first killed. That was in 1932. We got $75 per month for Linda, our child, and me. He had been a chemist and atomic bomb scientist and no one would insure him. I wanted a lump sum rather than the $75 per month but they wouldn't do it.

"Twice a year the government checked on me to make sure I hadn't remarried because then they could have stopped the payments. They used to come out to the house to check on me. I was working in the yard one day and the man came up to me and asked me to sign the papers saying I wasn't married yet. Well, I was hot and tired and I told him that he could put it down in his little black book that I was going to live to be 105 and never remarry and that someday they would be sorry they hadn't settled for a lump sum instead of bothering me. Well, they never came back again to check on me and I'm still collecting." (The narrator of this story is 80.)

Judy H. lived and worked overseas many years. She met several like-minded women, all single at the time, and they kept in touch, meeting once a year in one or another foreign country.

When these women returned to the United States they dispersed to different parts of the country but kept in contact by phone and mail. Little by little, most of them married, and Judy was happy for them, except for one.

Judy showed me the letter she'd received from this woman a few months after her marriage. It said that her new husband, a Baptist minister, had taken all the statuary she had collected from her travels, piled it all in the back yard and smashed it, declaring that the statues were "idolatrous."

The deed itself wasn't quite as horrible as what she wrote after her description of the incident. "But still, it's better than being single."

A business woman tells this story. "He came over to my house and I fixed this really nice dinner. Then he asked me over to his place for dinner. He placed a droopy salad in front of me and said that's all he'd fixed because he was on a diet. Later, he started bragging about how he likes being single because there's plenty of women willing to provide him with sex.

"I told him I'd found the same situation, that there's plenty of men around to provide all the sex I need. I told him I was real picky, however, and turned most of them down. He couldn't wait to get rid of me and hasn't called since."

Since the AIDS thing, I guess some men are cautious too. I got propositioned the other night by a man who said he was attracted to me "because I looked so clean." I really don't know how to take that, except I don't feel flattered.

In his book *The Divorce Decision* Gary Richmond, director of a single parents ministry at First Evangelical Free Church in Fullerton, California, tells of a woman who came to his office for advice. Her question: Should she take back her husband, a former pastor to whom she'd been married for 20 years and then divorced? Before she had divorced, he had been having an affair with this other woman, and when she confronted him with it, he hit her and knocked her to the floor. Now, four years later, he had contacted the first wife and she was considering taking him back. She told Richmond that the ex-husband's offer sounded better than the loneliness she was suffering without him.

HOW TO BE A BITCH AND OTHER SELF-ESTEEM BOOSTERS

"I was overweight, divorced, raising two kids on my own and attracting the attention of a healthy, intelligent, wealthy, powerful physician . . . It's every woman's dream."

—From an Associated Press story by Sharon Cohen on criminal proceedings against a physician accused of gross negligence, lewd conduct, rape and other offenses against more than a dozen women, mostly patients, some of whom were impregnated and had abortions by him.

I went to check up on my older friend Ruth in her mobile home park because I hadn't been able to reach her by phone for several weeks. She wasn't home so I knocked on the doors of her neighbors to ask about her whereabouts. One was an elderly man Ruth had told me about. She argued with him frequently, especially when he told her he didn't believe that she had never wanted to remarry after her husband died 30 years before. When I asked about her he stuck his head out the door and said, "You know, she don't like men."

VI

AIDS and Other Sex-Busters

Like it or not, sex can be dangerous. Today single women in particular have to rethink the importance and value of lust 'n' love in their lives.

It's too late, of course, to make a rational plan for taking control of your sex life when there's an eager new man in bed next to you. Before this happens, you might want to re-evaluate what you want from your sex life in light of recent social changes.

Two factors altered, perhaps forever, the terms under which we agree to have sex. One was the sexual revolution of the 1970s; the other was the onslaught of the acquired immunodeficiency syndrome (AIDS) epidemic in the decade that followed.

As Dana Brookins says, "Isn't it interesting that we got to this [liberated] point in our lives and up came AIDS. What a damn shame. We don't have to get pregnant now, but look what got dropped on us. Here we are with the freedom and we can't do anything with it."

At a publishers' convention I was talking to a magazine editor about this book. When I explained the premise and the fact that it included a chapter on sex issues for women up to age 100, he exclaimed, "Well, it's not such a problem for older women, though."

I asked what he meant by "older" and he sort of hemmed and hawed and said, "Well, those over . . . about 50," at which point I began laughing uproariously to keep from slugging him. Talk about the Stone Age. I should have let him know that it's men like him who make many women choose to remain single.

We're dealing with five main issues: (1) people of all ages are active sexually; (2) sex and love can be interchangeable; (3) AIDS is not age-specific; (4) both men and women enjoy sex, but they think about it and approach it differently; (5) AIDS isn't gender-specific, although it's more difficult for a man to get it from a woman than it is for a woman to get it from a man.

AIDS and other sexually transmitted diseases should be serious concerns for single people of both sexes. I once thought it would be women who set the standards for sexual behavior in this era of AIDS. That it would be women who would have to insist that men wear condoms. But I changed my thinking after listening to both men and women talk about how they are handling their sex lives these days.

The care that must be taken is an unwelcome change for many who miss the sense of abandonment sex can give—not necessarily in a promiscuous sense, but in the personal feeling of joy that good sex can bring. Part of my rethinking was the result of listening in on discussions such as one among a small group of writers, both male and female. One man said that he had found several women who refused to have sex using condoms even though he insisted on them. Then a woman said that she never would ask a man to use a condom. Not only did she believe the request would be rude, but she thought sex with a condom wouldn't be much fun. This woman said she would simply get to know her partner better first, and then she could "tell" if he was safe.

I could only gasp at her remarks, but they spoke volumes about just what health officials are warning: Too many people think they fall into the low-risk categories.

Another fallacy women sometimes fall for is that men over 50 are "safe." They can't picture these men as rompers in bed. I still hear women make comments like, "Oh, I know he's safe. He was married for many years and hasn't been single that long."

Ladies, that sweet-looking man with the balding pate may be sleeping with a different woman every night of the week, especially if she provides a home-cooked meal. Men his age were liberated long before we were. Back in the 1950s they got the message that anything-goes-if-you-can-get-it, but we females waited until the 1960s to get the same clue. Ultimately, of course, lots of us now over 40 who had bought into the belief that "nice girls don't" when we were younger, were delighted at the demise of the double standard.

Today, however, many researchers, sexologists and mental health experts believe that women were the heavy losers during the sexual revolution. Nevertheless, it may take a long time to evaluate what it did or didn't do for women.

Certainly the sexual revolution did acknowledge that the human female is every bit as sexual a creature as the male. I've talked to many level-headed women, still single, whose memories of the brief romances they had during the 1960s and 1970s are pleasant. They have no regrets, largely because they weren't in search of marriage partners. For others, however, one-night stands left something to be desired, especially if the woman believed that she'd found her knight in shining armor.

Some of the singles' organizations that sprouted up in the late 1970s also left something to be desired. During the early 1980s I wrote a three-part series on singles' groups for a newspaper in the suburbs of Los Angeles. In the course of my field work, I made every effort to see them as positive, especially since I was single myself. Unfortunately, my first impression of the dozen or so groups I researched never changed. I thought they were the worst way possible to meet someone of the opposite sex. A woman in her 30s used the term "meat markets"—one step beyond, but not above, most singles' bars.

After attending several singles' meetings, I became so depressed one night that I took another female reporter along for a different point of view. The function we attended was a dance sponsored by three different singles' groups. The reporter, who had just gone through a divorce of her own, wrote out her notes, turned them in and wouldn't speak to me for two weeks. "Yes, they're depressing," she had written. "If this is what I have to look forward to now that I'm divorced, I think I'll just end it before it gets worse."

Fortunately she didn't "end it," and now, years later, we can laugh about the experience. Looking back, we realize that we had picked up the feelings of lonely, desperate people who believed happiness was possible only when they can find the right person. Smart singles know this isn't true. They know that happiness comes from within, that it's elusive. They know that, yes, happiness is felt on occasion, but it is not a state anyone stays in very much of the time.

Singles' organizations are more sophisticated now; many offer videotapes and computer link-ups. I suspect, however, that the same old frenzy still surrounds the concept.

On the other hand, I also recognize that some of these services, including the plethora of singles' magazines and newsletters, do a remarkable service in getting people together. I'm always reminded that one of the most compatible couples I know, married 15 years with two small children, met through the personal ads in a newspaper.

Linda Olsen, a former Los Angeles psychologist, in the 1980s said dating services and singles' groups "are an attempt to restore the mating process [which has broken down with the rapidly changing society], but that they use junior high school rules."

Olsen, who has since married, acknowledges that as a single person she joined some singles' groups herself before deciding that they just didn't work. She had moved to California from another state for professional reasons and set about purposefully making friends and forming a strong support group. She considers this type of networking necessary for well-being.

Olsen pointed out that many of the people who attend singles' groups haven't settled the inner conflicts left over from recent divorces or widowhood. She found her salvation, she says, by joining special-interest groups like the Sierra Club, where she met people with values similar to her own. When she attended their meetings she found a mixture of members—of all ages, and all stages of life, married, never married, divorced and widowed.

These organizations met her needs to be involved in something that implemented her life goals. If she happened to meet someone along the way, fine. If not, her time had been spent doing something she enjoyed.

Meeting someone of the opposite sex isn't the only problem now, however. What to *do* with him is a bigger problem. AIDS has taken away most of the freedom and some of the fun. We may spend too much time bemoaning the fact that sex can be dangerous while listening raptly to what's happening out there in the sexual world. What we hear is glum: About 10,000 American women now have AIDS and more than 100,000 more women are infected with HIV (human immunodeficiency virus) that causes AIDS, according to the U.S. Center for Disease Control. In 1991, AIDS is expected to be the fifth leading cause of death for women of child-bearing age. Studies indicate that about one-third of these women will have contracted HIV infection through heterosexual contact; one-third through intravenous drug use; and for another one-third the source of infection will be unidentified.

Because there is such a long latency period between infection and appearance of symptoms, many people have a false sense of security. Others don't perceive themselves in danger because of their age, despite projections that by 1991 there will be 10,000 AIDS patients over the age of 60—people who probably became infected in their late 40s or early 50s.

Many others still believe AIDS is a disease primarily of gays and intravenous drug users, despite its spread among heterosexual monogamous couples who could have been infected as long as 12 years ago through blood transfusion or prior relationships.

The medical community has poured most of its energies into finding a cure or effective inoculation against a disease that has infected between 1 and 1.5 million people. From 78 to 100 percent of them will come down with AIDS within 15 years.

This information might seem frightening, but it doesn't eliminate the fact that most men and women will continue to have sexual relations no matter what.

"The days are over for intelligent people to meet someone and go to bed with them that night," says psychology professor Marcia Lasswell. "Men and women have to realize that to get involved sexually, they should become friends first. It's not prudish. It's just wise. Furthermore, if they are going to be involved sexually, they should ask for sexual exclusivity. Of course they can practice what is called 'safe sex,' but I once heard Theresa Crenshaw, M.D., who was on former President Reagan's commission on the HIV epidemic, ask an audience of about 2,000 marriage and family therapists how many of them had ever talked to their clients about safe sex and using condoms. All raised their hands. Then she asked how many would have sex with someone they knew had AIDS, even if they were the lover of their dreams, and even if they used a condom. Not a single hand went up.

"You're pretty desperate if you expose yourself to AIDS in order to get a man," adds Lasswell. "You have to ask yourself, 'Would you really want to have sex, even with the protection of a condom, with someone who had AIDS?'"

The major problem, according to health professionals, isn't getting people to use condoms, but to get them simply to *talk*, openly and honestly, about sex and condoms and AIDS.

Some health professionals say that warning women of the dangers of the epidemic isn't enough. It's important to make the threat of AIDS real in their minds, but behavior-intervention techniques are also needed. Successful behavioral modification lies in altering certain patterns of behavior rather than changing entire lifestyles or frightening people away from sex. "People respond better to choice than they do to simplistic, moralistic approaches," says Marshall Becker, professor of health behavior and associate dean at the School of Public Health at the University of Michigan. Becker serves on the National Research Council's Committee on AIDS Research and the Social, Behavioral and Statistical Sciences.

"Just saying no to sex doesn't appeal to the majority of people," says Becker. "But there are lots of methods available that will change people's attitude and behaviors. One of them is to change the actual situation in which the behavior takes place. An easy example of this is taking ashtrays out of rooms to discourage smoking. People looked around and found no place to put the ashes. With AIDS you can do things like making condoms much more available and more obvious. Make them easier to acquire."

Becker also advocates a change in the setting in which singles meet. He believes the arrangement should be less casual, that society should provide support systems for introducing men and women.

"We can also encourage group pressure to change what we consider to be the norm," he says. "We can make it normative to ask certain questions of the person you're with. Another powerful behavior modification method is 'value attitude conflict,' whereby we show people they are acting with an inappropriate attitude. Examples are the smokers who say 'It's my life.' We can show them how their early death is going to affect other members of the family, such as children and grandchildren.

"What I'm saying is that, for God's sake, let's be a little more sophisticated in dealing with AIDS rather than falling back on fear," he says. "Because people resent that."

Some medical professionals recommend HIV testing during the period when heterosexual couples are establishing a relationship. Results are available in ten days to two weeks. The drawback to such testing, however, is that infection obtained within the past six months might not yet show up.

For now, at least, it isn't practical, says Deborah Cohen, M.D., assistant clinical professor of family medicine at the University of Southern California School of Medicine.

The usual test identifies only people who haven't developed antibodies to HIV. If someone tests positive, then that person must be tested again, usually with the standard Western Blot Test, which is more sophisticated. If the WBT is positive, then the person is considered HIV-positive.

The problem with the tests is that once a person has to be celibate for periods ranging from two to six months to be sure of a negative result. "In other words, if a person was exposed to AIDS in January, it might not show up until July on the test," says Cohen.

"It just depends on the people. How honest they are. What their habits are. You just can't really be sure. If they don't do drugs or sleep with anyone else after the test, you're okay. But who's to know?" asks Cohen, adding that research has shown that men, especially, will lie in order to get sex.

"An individual only knows for sure what he or she is doing. The only way a single woman who isn't committing to a relationship can be safe is to use condoms and on top of that to use a spermicide," Cohen advises, adding that deep kissing hasn't been shown to be a problem but that oral sex can be dangerous.

Cohen says the people who believe they are at the lowest risk are actually at high risk because they frequently use no protection of any sort. "People who have multiple sex partners and who believe their partners are clean 'because they can just tell' are at the highest risk of all," she says.

Testing is a good idea for your own peace of mind. If you were sexually active after 1978, you may want to be tested, especially if you believe you had sexual relations with someone who was an intravenous drug user or a bisexual.

Anyone who is at high risk should be tested, according to the Centers for Disease Control. Knowing of the condition early on, before it manifests itself into full-blown AIDS, will give a person time to develop health habits that may postpone the onset of the disease.

"Formerly married" or "married" still doesn't mean safe, as attested to in Amity Pierce Buxton's book *The Other Side of the Closet*. Buxton, a northern California therapist, was married for more than 20 years to a man who eventually acknowledged that he had been leading a double life. He was gay.

Health professionals caution that sex partners are, in effect, having sex with every man or woman the other partner has been with. Even if your man is heterosexual, you're still at risk. On the other hand, *you* may present a risk to your partner.

Cohen is among the growing number of professionals who believe much more education and publicity on condom use is needed among the general population as well as among teens and college-age young people.

Elizabeth Bacon hosted a "condom party" sponsored by her local Planned Parenthood organization. "This woman from Planned Parenthood came out to the house and showed the women how to use condoms," she says. "We brought bananas and cucumbers and practiced. It was as simple as that. It was like, 'We've got a problem and here is one solution.' Single women of all ages attended the gathering, along with one married woman who said it sounded like fun."

But being forced to take such precautions hasn't been fun. Many women say that they not only don't like to use condoms, but they question their safety. In addition, most of us shy away from discussing AIDS as a very real sexual issue, and we haven't developed the language to talk about it with potential sexual partners.

Mara Adelman, communications professor at Northwestern University, was one of several speakers at a symposium in San Diego in 1990 called "Negotiating Safe Sex: Social Science Theory and Research." Reports at the symposium indicate that AIDS is definitely reshaping the singles' scene. "Our notions of what sexuality is are going to change," she says. "Traditional penetration has been the end-all-be-all of the sexual act. Sexuality is being redefined," she says.

This redefinition is still on the drawing board, but today the artists aren't just lovers, they are sociologists, physicians, mental health professionals, anthropologists and other scientists.

"Now that people are dying of AIDS, it's suddenly okay to discuss sexuality openly," Adelman says.

"Safe sex is an oxymoron because abandonment and caution at the same time are incongruent," she says. "It goes against our romantic notion of sex because you have something that is planned linked with something that is spontaneous. Sex is associated with pleasure and it's private. AIDS pits two basic human goals against one another—avoiding death and seeking love."

Safe sex not only goes against our traditional views of sex, it requires that we talk about a playful, creative brain act using our logical left brains. "People know that sex isn't about being safe," says social scientist Lynn Miller of the University of Southern California.

Nor does sex involve discussion. The decision to have sex is usually nonverbal. "How do you incorporate the verbal act of condom use?" asks Miller. "Unless you're incredibly skilled, it's very difficult. And at the same time you're trying not to offend your partner. If you want to have a long-term relationship, you're concerned with the image you're projecting. Some people suggest bringing up the subject of AIDS over dinner in a restaurant. But at that stage of the relationship, you may not have established that you are going to have sex. There is simply no cookbook with the strategies to use. It's a moment-by-moment situation."

With the help of B. Ann Bettencourt and students at the University of Southern California, Miller has identified 101 obstacles to safe sex.

The top ten: (1) the heat of the moment; (2) talking about safe sex; (3) the act of presenting or buying condoms; (4) the condom is unromantic; (5) pressure not to use a condom; (6) anticipating a partner's problem (using the condom); (7) difficulty with the condom; (8) rejection of the partner (for insisting on a condom); (9) loss of partner (risk of losing the relationship); (10) availability of a condom (immediate access to one).

Adelman says she has produced a video for couples on how to discuss safe sex—it deals primarily with condom use. "People were uncomfortable viewing the video so imagine how uncomfortable they'd be discussing alternatives to intercourse, like mutual masturbation," she says. "Even people who have known each other for a long time aren't comfortable with alternatives to intercourse."

Adelman and others who deal professionally with sexual issues believe that AIDS is redefining sex, and that new outlooks on sex are already in the making. These new attitudes will produce a view of sexual intercourse that is less phallically centered; pornography for women will become more acceptable, especially that made by and for women; condoms will become a common courtesy; there will be much more discussion about sexuality; and new ways of giving sexual pleasure will become popular, such as mutual masturbation, massage and telephone sex. "Romance novels are already getting juicier," says Adelman.

Elizabeth Grauerholz, assistant professor of sociology at Purdue University, says it's quite possible that the threat of AIDS will push more women into getting married if they've already been considering it. Singles who are content with their lifestyles, however, won't be pushed into marriage just because of a general fear of AIDS. In the meantime, unless condoms are used for sexual activity that puts one at risk, experts say abstinence is the answer.

One alternative for single women, of course, is masturbation, and there is no doubt more women are shedding their inhibitions about this solitary form of sexual gratification. Of course, female masturbation wasn't invented during the sexual revolution. It just became a subject that was discussed openly. Feminist Margaret Adams described it succinctly in her 1976 book *Single Blessedness*: "This is a universally accessible mode of sexual activity that deals very adequately with the physiological tensions of sex and as such has been a useful built-in resource for unattached single individuals. . . . Its disadvantage is that until recently it has been considered a shameful aberration, colored with considerable guilt and incurring a good many self-doubts. Even today it is relegated to a second-class place in the sexual hierarchy, the general view being that it is resorted to only when better prospects are not at hand."

Someone with concerns about AIDS told me, "Yeah, sex can be dangerous to your health. You like sex? Fall in love with your hand."

Celibacy has also become more common. It is being lauded more today than it was at the turn of the century when large numbers of women were proclaiming their independence.

In the early 1900s, politicians, health practitioners and the clergy sounded the alarm about the "new women" who were staying celibate instead of marrying; these arbiters of morality considered the choice of celibacy a symptom of the sexual disease called frigidity.

About this same time Freudian theories were being embraced in certain circles. Here the wish to be single and remain celibate was blamed on childhood trauma and arrested development.

By the 1920s, women who chose to remain single were viewed as masculinized females or lesbians. Women who shared an emotional closeness that eluded the male gender were suspected of deviance—a suspicion that still exists today.

It has always surprised me (but shouldn't, I suppose) that many women who have instigated divorce have been asked by their ex-husbands if they have become lesbian. It's as if that particular accusation is the worst thing they can throw at the woman who has rejected him.

Margaret Adams was once called "unsexed" by a columnist because of her feminist views. Today, however, the other side is being heard. Erica Jong's latest book, *Any Woman's Blues*, pushes the message that it's better to be celibate and gain your own identity than to count on getting it from a man. Jong is the author of *Fear of Flying*, a seventies novel that promoted sexual liberation and also sold 10 million copies in 22 languages.

In line with these new ideas on celibacy, more than 400 men and women have joined the National Chastity Association, formed in 1988 by Mary Meyer, a divorced mother of two. The nonreligious organization acts as an informal dating service and support group. One of its goals, which may not appeal to women who choose to be single, is that members eventually marry. Still, the organization points out the growing acceptability of celibacy.

Author William F. Kraft says in *Sexual Dimensions of the Celibate Life* that healthy forms of love, except marriage, exclude genital behavior. He also says that living alone is a "powerful test of love and sexuality." Kraft believes chastity promotes and nourishes healthy sexuality because unchaste sex is "oriented around self-satisfaction."

Author Gabrielle Brown writes in *The New Celibacy* that there are "really no instructions necessary for becoming celibate. All that is necessary is to decide to be celibate," because it is a mental decision.

But she cautions: "To be celibate as opposed to frustrated or martyred, one must make a conscious choice for a good reason—on behalf of one's own personal fulfillment. And once we have chosen to be celibate for a time, the same principle applies to remaining celibate."

Still, Brown doesn't advocate vowing to stay celibate. As with a diet, it's much better to tell yourself to just cut down on your eating rather than to stop eating.

Many of the women I interviewed said they had become celibate since they became fully aware of the threat of AIDS. They seem to fall into several categories, depending on their ages. Those under 35 say they don't sleep around anymore, but have, or would be willing to develop, a sexual relationship with a single man. Many (but not all) who are older, and who may have been married or widowed, say that using condoms and negotiating their way into healthy sexual relationships doesn't seem worth the bother. Some in the second category feel that what is necessary to develop a healthy sexual relationship with a man today smacks too much of commitment.

They realize this leaves them in a quandary. They have become too independent to want a committed relationship, and yet they enjoy the company of men and aren't prudes when it comes to sex.

Then there are women like Marjory Stoneman-Douglas, the Florida environmentalist, who acknowledges she gave up sex at an early age in favor of devoting herself solely to her work. She says, "Sex isn't worth all the bother."

One single woman in her early 50s, who previously had an active sex life, said, "I haven't even dated for nearly two years. That's unnatural for me. AIDS interfered. Condoms just aren't worth it. It's a mind-set. I've been exposed to a lot of men. Dated all the time, had lots of male friends. Now I'm more comfortable with myself and I keep busy all the time. I know now I will never have time to hear all the music I like, read all the books I've missed, and eat all the fudge I want. It's almost a rude awakening. Since I realized at 52 that I won't be able to do everything I want to do, I decided to spend some time with myself. I can go to bed at 8 o'clock and read and know I'm not missing anything more important."

A woman in her early 40s said, "Condoms are an answer, if not the best. It's what we've got. I don't know if using them is inhibiting, but AIDS has certainly inhibited me. I've been celibate for a long time. I don't do sex casually. Never have. It's the old thing of 'I have to be in love.' Occasionally, though, I used to fall in love for a week. But not anymore."

A woman who just turned 50 says, "The last date I had was 10 years ago. I would hate to be young now. When I was young you could catch some amazing things—crabs and genital warts. I managed to steer clear of those. I know women who didn't. I also steered clear of gonorrhea and syphilis. God had a hell of a sense of humor when he invented sex, huh?"

It seems paradoxical that medical literature keeps telling women past 40 that a healthy sex life keeps you healthier and happier. "They say it keeps the juices flowing," says sociologist Barbara Cambridge. "Well, I say estrogen does that too. So we tell menopausal women if they are fearful of AIDS to pop an estrogen pill."

Unfortunately society infers that something's wrong with you if you prefer celibacy over sex and its risks. This is nothing new, as early feminists found out, but now women must not only face name-calling for their feminist views, they must be prepared to deal with other name-calling when they insist on "safe sex."

AIDS is the most dangerous sex-buster right now, but it isn't the only sexually transmitted disease (STD). The others, such as genital warts and herpes, have simply taken a back seat. They injure, but they don't kill. Not surprisingly, condoms are recommended for prevention of these diseases. Studies have shown that the use of condoms cuts down on all STDs. Of course, there are treatments for the old standbys syphilis and gonorrhea, but prevention is still better than treatment.

There are many promising cures, vaccines and preventive drugs on the horizon for AIDS, but it may be years before they become reality. In the meantime, women need to enlighten themselves about a disease that can kill them just as readily as it can an IV drug user or a sexually active homosexual who doesn't take proper precautions.

Elaine Showalter says in *Sexual Anarchy* that the good news might be that syphilis once caused terror, illness and death, but a cure was finally found, as it may be for AIDS.

Showalter and other feminists believe that the AIDS epidemic will force the issue of sexuality into the open for a long, overdue airing. Then we will recognize the sexual diversity among people, and become better acquainted with our own sexuality and that of our partners.

For help and information contact the National AIDS Information Clearinghouse, P.O. Box 6003, Rockville, Maryland, 20850, 800-458-5231.

VII

Loneliness, Depression, and Other Normalities Like Friends and Celebrations

Loneliness

Women who choose to be single thrive alone because they're good at being alone, because they like themselves and because they know that being married doesn't preclude loneliness. If they were previously married, they enjoyed periods of solitude and frequently wished they had more of it. They know what Virginia Woolf meant when she said that every women needs a room of her own.

I was reminded by a male married friend that loneliness isn't the domain of singles, nor of women who choose not to marry or remarry. Two years ago, novelist Joe Citro moved to a rural area of Vermont hoping the change would give more uninterrupted time to write. His wife's job was 25 miles distant and often required that she be away for days at a time. Citro, author of several thrillers including *The Unseen* and *Dark Twilight*, found instead that his absolute isolation had an undesired effect on productivity.

Because I live alone and write at home in my mountain cabin, he asked me if I ever suffered from loneliness. "You bet I do," I answered. "But I consider it the price I pay for choosing to live as I do." We decided to correspond on the subject.

He has since written saying, "Regardless of where we live, writing, by nature, is a lonely profession. I think we suffer from not having a work place like REAL people. If we could grumble around the water cooler, harangue beside the coffee machine, rant in the lounge or go out for drinks after work to piss 'n' moan, well, maybe we'd be okay.

"The biggest part of my problem has simply been an adjustment to a major lifestyle change," he went on. "Used to be I'd go out to lunch once or twice a week with my pals, or if I hit a snag or felt antsy I could go to a book or video store. Now pals and stores are 40 minutes away! A one-hour break for lunch usually costs me a minimum of three hours.

"One concession I've made is that I now take Friday afternoons off. I drive into Burlington, have lunch, take care of errands, mess around and generally relax. Then I join [my wife] Linda after work for drinks, dinner, socializing, maybe a movie or whatever. This new routine is a good change of pace. It marks the end of the week with something rewarding and mildly festive.

"In general I feel better adjusted to my situation now than I did when we first spoke about loneliness in California."

Single women who are having problems with loneliness can take a lesson from Citro. He recognized his problem and did something about it.

Many health professionals said loneliness is bad for

health, and it's true, but that has nothing to do with marital status. I suppose that if you let your worries about loneliness become chronic, and if you don't take pleasure in the freedom you can find in solitude, then loneliness is bad for you.

"Some people are more couple-oriented than others," acknowledges psychologist Marcia Lasswell. "For them, it would be tough to be single."

But there are few health experts, ministers and therapists who say it's better to be in a bad relationship than none at all because single people are lonely. Any happy single knows that experts who mouth such nonsense are either biased against singles, have hang-ups of their own about spending time alone, or simply don't understand the difference between solitude and loneliness. They certainly aren't aware that healthy singles are adept at forming strong friendships and support groups.

Some research has implied that it's healthier to be married than to be single because of the alleged isolation involved in going it alone. When pinned down, those same researchers will say they meant "lack of support groups" rather than a husband. Virtually all the hardy single people I know personally and those I interviewed, have large support networks that include family members and friends.

Psychiatrist Rege Stewart says she sees lots of women who blame all their unhappiness on their single status. She also sees married women who blame all their unhappiness on being married and who say if they could just get out of their marriages everything would be wonderful.

It could be that the American cult of individualism is actually the culprit. Many who, for a variety of reasons, fail to make friends or to cherish the emotions of closeness with other human beings, use this philosophy as an excuse. Nineteenth-century playwright Henrik Ibsen said that the strongest man in the world is he who stands most alone. This belief and not the choice to remain single is what promotes loneliness.

Loneliness, a universal human condition, can be defined as an unpleasant mood or feeling caused by the discrepancy between what people want from relationships and what they perceive they are getting from those relationships.

Ami Rokach, psychologist at the Ontario Correctional Institute in Ontario, Canada, in an article called "The Experience of Loneliness: A Tri-Level Model" (*Journal of Psychology*), writes: "Man is, and has always been, a lonely and separate entity. The struggle to escape that fate is probably as old as mankind. Although the human race is made up of many different people, and despite the many divisive forces among us such as language, culture, religious beliefs, and socioeconomic levels, there are some fundamental similarities. One of those similarities is our yearning for love, acceptance, and understanding. Because reality does not always work according to our desires, we go through life experiencing frustration, restlessness, and loneliness."

As society becomes faster paced, as people turn more to electronics for amusement, and as we disperse to far corners of the country leaving long-time friends and family behind, the potential for isolation increases.

Since approximately 50 percent of our health status is linked to the way we live, an emphasis on independence isn't all that healthy, says Milton Miller, M.D., professor of psychiatry at the University of California at Los Angeles.

Miller says that socially isolated people have two to three times the risk of premature death as those who are involved with other people. Death from cardiovascular disease is strikingly high among recently widowed men 55 and older; 40 percent higher within the first six months of widowhood than that of married men the same age.

Sociologist Janet Giele believes that the way men are raised and socialized encourages them to put all their emotional eggs in one basket. "Men tend to have one intimate relationship," she says. If a woman loses her mate, she's likely to go ahead and live a long life, while a man isn't as likely to.

So it isn't that single women don't need people. They do. The difference is, they know it. People who say they don't need people are telling a bit of a lie. Human beings are social animals, and scientists have found that people who own up to this need, not only live longer, but are healthier and happier. It's incumbent on both singles and non-singles to spend time nurturing and developing friendships.

In the past, male and female singles were lumped together statistically. Newer research shows that women survive much better as singles than do men. Part of the reason is that they know how to nurture, and do so in their everyday lives, including nurturing themselves. Women tend to develop a circle of friends, and are free to hug and touch other human beings, including children. This gives them the tactile stimulation of nurturing.

Men, too, need nurturing to survive, but they don't know how to nurture themselves, so they turn to the women in their lives.

Men and women also handle loneliness differently. According to Joseph Stokes and Ira Levin, psychologists at the University of Illinois at Chicago, men function best in groups. They place value on friends who share similar attitudes, activities and interests. A man's loneliness can be predicted by the number of friends in his social network—not individuals, but *groups* of people. Women, however, place greater emphasis on emotional sharing and intimacy, with fewer but closer friends.

These patterns originate in early childhood. A man's sense of self develops through an alliance with a gang or group of boys where solidarity is highly valued. Girls develop through deeper relationships with female friends where close, intimate exchanges are valued.

Men who maintain alliances with groups of males, and women who form strong individual friendships tend to be less lonely than men and women without these relationships, according to a paper presented by Stokes and Levin at the annual convention of the American Psychological Association in 1985.

People's attitudes can predict whether or not they will suffer loneliness. Those who are depressed, neurotic, have low self-esteem or a cynical world-view are more likely to suffer loneliness. Cynicism and rejection of others may turn off potential friends, and make it more difficult for some people to develop the friendships they so desperately need.

Loneliness, as any successful single knows, can't be blamed on some guy "out there," or on a particular group that makes you feel uncomfortable. Loneliness comes from within. In other words, a person can be in a crowded bar, boardroom or bedroom, and still feel lonely. Mental health experts agree that people need to develop social networks with individuals, groups or volunteer organizations, and to work hard at maintaining individual friends in order to overcome loneliness.

Jerry Lee, a research psychologist at Loma Linda University Medical Center, says that if he were a practicing psychologist, he would recommend that his clients get out and work as volunteers. Getting your mind off yourself and focusing on the needs of others, even if it's just listening to a friend, helps to overcome loneliness and promotes good health, he says.

So clearly, loneliness isn't a curse afflicting only single women. It can affect anyone, either chronically or temporarily. Some research shows that people who suffer severe bouts of loneliness were given little nurturing as children and that they are always looking for someone to fill up the empty feeling within.

To take control of their own well-being, psychologist Marcia Lasswell says a woman should take stock of her friends or acquaintances and consider who can be turned into close friends. "At first she must devote more than 50 percent of the giving and nurturing in these relationships," Lasswell emphasizes. "The woman needs to take inventory and find out things she's interested in and pursue them so that she becomes a more interesting person. She needs to overcome the fear of going places alone, and that includes travel." Lasswell cautions that when she says "travel" she doesn't mean singles-only cruises or trips (see chapter 9).

Some Tips for Avoiding Loneliness

—Try to balance your life between work, outings and social relationships.
—Place a high value on your social relationships and spend time cultivating them.

- —Be open to meeting people with different interests than yours.
- —Redecorate your home. Make yourself a particular place of comfort to perform special activities.
- —Reflect on how you enjoy doing something in particular, such as walking, journal writing, or painting.
- —Volunteer your time to an organization.
- —Try something that you've never done before, such as cross-country skiing, square-dancing or cake-decorating.
- —Take a class that's not in your usual area of interest.
- —Do something outrageous.

All these take time and energy, but may well be worth the effort.

While I was walking with a friend one day, she said, "I wish I had time to walk everyday like you do." I turned to her and said, "I don't 'have' the time. I 'make' the time."

We all make time for things that are important to us. If you watch a lot of television, as I know this friend does, and you want to make time for something else, then you simply give up watching television. It's a choice, like the choice not to be lonely. You can't sit back and wish loneliness away. You have to take action, and, yes, it takes time and risks.

As Glenna McAnish says: "I realize that people who are lonely and afraid find it difficult to say to someone else, 'Oh, come to my house,' because there is always that fear of rejection. But it can't get worse. If you are already alone and then you are rejected, you're still alone. It didn't get any worse!"

Be realistic, though, about what all this activity can do

for you. If basic responsibility for happiness lies within, then as a single you must develop the self-esteem to live alone. No one person, friend, acquaintance, organization or living arrangement is going to make you feel good about yourself. That also comes from within. Life doesn't hand out self-esteem on a silver platter. For some, it's a lifetime struggle to achieve some pride and self-respect. Still, just because it's a struggle doesn't mean you should give up, or give in to the notion that someone else is going to take away your loneliness.

Friends

Women who are single by choice know they need friends and family to live a full life. Until the beginning of the twentieth century, family provided all the support most people needed. As American migration patterns caused increasing family dispersal, friendships became as important as family.

But making friends is tricky. It's not something that can be done overnight or with a first meeting. Making friends takes time and nurturing. And ironically, those people who make the least demands on their friends are the ones who make friends most easily.

John Leonard is quoted in *Friends and Friends of Friends* as saying, "It takes a long time to grow an old friend." But before a friendship can grow old, it has to be made. This is not easy, so it shouldn't come as a surprise that an organization called Buddy Brokers was born. Designed along the lines of a singles' group that matches couples, this one matches potential friends of the same sex. It was started by a married couple, Kate and Dane Teague of San Jose, California. They believe it's more difficult to meet potential friends with likes, dislikes and interests similar to our own than it is to find a mate.

A mate is a mate, but there are many different levels of friendships:

—*Acquaintances.* Coworkers, some neighbors, old school chums, owners of businesses we frequent, parents of our children's friends, friends of friends, and people who frequent organizations to which we belong. All of these people may, eventually, become close friends.

—*Comrades or confederates.* These are people who might share something in common with us, perhaps a hobby, work, age or a problem. Confederates might be found in a particular type of support group such as a weight-loss organization or an A.A. meeting. People from this group may become close friends but usually they just become casual acquaintances or used-to-be-friends after the activity is completed or cancelled. Sometimes a temporary friendship will develop between a stronger member of the group and someone who relies on that person. This type of friendship often ends when the weaker one becomes stronger.

—*Deep friendships.* These friends come in all sizes and shapes and aren't necessarily interested in the same things we are, although there are usually some shared interests in work or play. A person can have more than one close friend, but not more than several. Best friends were well depicted in the movie *Beaches*, with Bette Midler and Barbara Hershey as women who stayed friends through thick and thin, differing viewpoints, illness and death.

Our own deep friendships may not be as dramatic, but they add meaning to our lives. Losing a best friend can be as devastating as the breakup of a marriage. Like marriage, friendships need tender loving care, as well as flexibility. Recently, on the way home from a trip, I had a silly argument with a friend. I was driving and we disagreed about the mileage from one point to another. Soon we were screaming and for about 20 miles we didn't speak. Finally my friend said, "It's nice we're such good friends we're not afraid to argue with one another."

These deep or intimate friendships, as they're sometimes called, defy analysis. The reasons why two people can share their deepest emotions and thoughts can't be put under a microscope. Sometimes a crisis draws people together. Sometimes it's a shared sense of joy over certain life events.

Some people have different types of close friends. One shares an understanding of your belief system. You can talk to another about your love life. To another you can rant and rave about the inconsistencies of life.

We give best friends spaces of understanding. We tolerate foibles in them that we wouldn't in another. Our love is unconditional. Best friends are dependable, they make us feel at home. We can let our guard down with them.

We never know when a friendship is going to drop in on us—a new one or an old one. Recently my daughter Julie called from an area where I used to live with the news that Marie, an old acquaintance of mine, had died. She'd been in one of the first writing groups I'd belonged to. As we went our separate ways, we'd stayed in contact with an occasional letter or card at Christmas.

Immediately after my daughter hung up, another one of

the same writing group members called and we arranged to meet at the funeral of our mutual friend. Marie had been one of those wonderfully outrageous people who are sometimes larger than life. At her funeral, I recounted to Marie's son one of her sayings that had stayed with me—"Life really isn't that much fun for those who just tiptoe through the tulips."

Marie was a good friend, not my best friend, but she'd shared an important part of my life. My joining the writing group had followed on the heels of my first venture back to college, which ultimately led to a writing career. She was there for me during a transitional part of my life.

Most of the single women I interviewed have close friends, as well as more distant friends.

When I divorced nearly 12 years ago, my very best friend was the wife of a fellow worker of my ex-husband's. We'd gone camping together for 19 years and shared the joys and anxieties of raising our children from infancy to near adulthood. When my marriage ended, so did our relationship. She absolutely avoided me and I was crushed.

A few years later, after I'd established myself in a profession, she called and said she really missed my friendship, but I was never able to regain that intimacy with her. Our paths had taken different turns.

Even among acquaintances, a change in status can change a relationship. The last five years of their marriage, Betty Wold and her husband were invited to a friend's large Christmas party. The year she was divorced, no invitation came, nor ever again, even though the person giving the party was a friend.

As we get older, it often becomes more difficult to make

new friends and we may lose some of our old ones. This is true whether we are married or single. "My friendships are now kind of down because so many of them have died," says Audrey Phillips. "I'm 87 and I've outlived a lot of them."

Some of the single women I've interviewed are outgoing and find it easy to meet new people. Some of them claim to be shy. Still all have developed strong support groups, and seem able to strike up easy conversations with strangers and people they've just met.

Most of the happy singles I know have a knack for telling good stories. They're especially good at telling jokes on themselves. They keep up with what's going on and have a wonderful way of laughing at the world's inconsistencies and at themselves. All are expert listeners and storytellers. They make great conversationalists, but there's more to great conversation than witty utterances. You've got to put your heart into it. Great conversationalists are truly concerned about the person they're talking with and what that person has to say. Because they're good at picking up cues, they quickly discover the other person's interests. They are curious about new subjects and they're not afraid to ask questions, which flatters the person to whom they're talking. They are participants in conversation rather than passive listeners.

They don't pepper the conversation with inattentive rejoinders such as "uh-huh." Nor do they try to grab the spotlight with machine-gun questions, or try to impress other people with their expertise.

Rather, they focus on the person and what is being said at that moment, as if that individual and that conversation are the most important things in their lives.

Being a good listener is only part of the picture. People who refuse to reveal their feelings and emotions can be boring.

Keeping talk flowing requires the ability to listen at appropriate times, yes. But it also means contributing. To brighten your conversational skills, experts recommend that you do the following:

—Decide ahead of time to be interested in the other person.
—Listen for cues in that person's conversation that tell you what is interesting or important to him or her.
—Respond to this free information by giving acknowledgment and asking a question about it.
—Feel free to ask that the other person repeat what they have just said.
—Be careful with your use of judgmental words like "should," "ought," "must" and "have to." They destroy communication.
—Watch out for overuse of all-inclusive words such as "always," "never," "nobody," "everybody" and "every time."
—Don't repeat irritating phrases such as "you know."
—Add words and phrases that add sparkle to conversation, including "I feel," "I want" and "because."
—Avoid sentences that start with "you." It's often better to use "we."
—Avoid body language that destroys conversation such as rubbing your nose, pulling an ear, shifting weight from one foot to another, rocking while sitting, pacing while standing, jingling stuff in your pockets, twirling a strand of hair or cracking your knuckles.
—Let the other person know you don't know it all. Seek their opinion and advice.

- Occasionally ask for clarification on a point made by the other person.
- Don't try to impress others with your expertise.
- Start off with simple subjects rather than trying to reshape world events.
- Read a variety of periodicals or utilize radio and television for interesting topics.
- Use anecdotes when explaining something. Even tell funny and humiliating tales about yourself.

Bear in mind that even great conversationalists have down times. It's unrealistic to expect to sparkle in every discussion. But even when a great conversationalist isn't in top form, she can still be interesting and interested. She can listen from the heart.

"Let me live in a house by the side of the road and be a friend to man," wrote Sam Walter Foss, nineteenth-century American librarian and poet. This could as easily have been written by and for women.

Author Chambers-Schiller writes in her book *Liberty, A Better Husband*, that the friendships of women in the eighteenth and nineteenth centuries provided "validations, affirmation and nurturing." Friendships today provide much the same, especially for women who choose to be single.

A friend of mine in her fifties, long divorced and among those who chose to remain single, recalls that early in her marriage, before she went out on her own, she used to think that men were more interesting than women.

Reflecting on her transition from housewife to noted author and professor, she says that, of course, in the early years of her marriage most men *were* more interesting because they worked outside the home and held power. Once she got out into the world and met women who also "held power," her allegiance shifted. Many women now past the age of 50 once held similar views, but today they cherish their friendships with women.

Until a woman—especially a single woman—realizes the value of other women, she can't love herself enough to have the self-esteem it takes to make it on her own. She'll always be looking for a man to "complete" her own inadequacies.

Ironically, once a woman has established herself as an equal to men, and can enjoy the company of women as much as that of men, then she's more ready for marriage than at any time before.

How much better to enter into a relationship with a man because you truly like to be with him, rather than to fill in some missing part of yourself.

"There's simply no problem meeting men out there if you're willing to go look for them, and I at times have set out to find them," says De Creasy. If a woman wants a man there are ways to get one. You meet them through friends, church, family or any other type of network.

"I know some women who are recently divorced and they are out man-prowling. Their only idea of being complete is to be with a man at all times or to have a man in their lives at all times. "There's just too much going on in my life for me to be that way," she says. "Right now, aside from my work, I'm involved in theater, with my friends, taking a real estate class, reading, and I'm learning sign language. I couldn't take care of a husband right now. You just can't have it all."

Choosing singleness is probably easier today for women because our work, which provides most of us with a certain amount of socializing with coworkers, is more secure than that of women of earlier generations. Women are now accepted into the work force in occupations that used to be the domain of men.

Making work your life, however, can also be dangerous. Some single women say they know others who have simply substituted careers for husbands. "Successful single women know they need to diversify and have many interests."

Sometimes single women find it tough hanging onto married couples or even married friends. The truth is, bachelor men are more frequently invited to functions with couples only. Married couples just having a simple dinner with their family will frequently invite a bachelor friend of the husband's. The single women won't get as many invitations from either the wife or husband.

Stormy Sandquist, a New Mexico artist, says that since turning 50 she receives more invitations from her married friends than she did before. "It's as if the older I get the safer they think I am," she said.

Ironically, few women who choose to be single would be remotely interested in a married man, much less the husbands of any of their friends. For one thing, friendship usually is too precious to risk by flirting with someone else's husband. For another, most independent women have access to enough single men who aren't married. As Brookins puts it, "Who would want any of those married duffers anyway?"

The other side of the coin is that, yes, it does happen, but the threat is still less likely to come from a friend. A married woman has more to fear from a neighbor, a husband's coworker or a prostitute than she does from a friend.

Another misconception is that increasing age brings with it a feeling of safety. I'm reminded of an incident that happened several years ago. My then-husband, a police officer, came home from work one day laughing about a shooting that had taken place at a senior citizens' mobile home park. An 80-year-old wife had shot a 79-year-old woman in the arm. The younger woman had been messing around with the first woman's 78-year-old husband. I was quite young at the time and my first thought was, "How extraordinary!" In my youthful naivete, I believed lust ended where middle age began.

I know now that lust doesn't end at any particular age. As before, behavior is a matter of decency. There is dignity in being a "true single," someone who isn't so desperate that she would stoop low enough to stalk the husband of one of her friends.

Lois Langland says that even if you choose to go it alone, no one makes it completely alone. "There are always friends and support systems," she says. "You recognize what you need and you work at making friends; you don't just lie back and let it happen. You can live alone and not be lonely. I think our need for people comes from our long dependency as infants. You feel you will literally die without somebody, and in fact that was the case when you were little. This need to bond is strong, but there are many ways of bonding."

Celebrate

"Oh blessed rage for order," wrote the poet Wallace Stevens. Rituals and celebrations help provide that order. They also force us out of lonely ruts. Health experts say human beings have a need to celebrate and take part in rituals. Singles need it as much as families do.

Celebrations and rituals give us a breather from the routine of daily living. They renew our faith and joy in who we are and where we belong. They furnish a sense of order when it seems there is none.

"Celebrations and rituals, no matter how insignificant they appear, are heavy with meaning," says Carlfred Broderick, a University of Southern California sociologist and psychologist. "They provide roots and foster a deeper sense of purpose and meaning in our lives. As well as giving our lives order, the touchstone of mental health, these special markers allow us to break the rules and to roleplay, which reduces stress."

Celebrations such as Halloween allow people to shed their daily facade. "We can be foolish on Halloween, and it's okay," says anthropologist Don Brenneis of Pitzer College in Claremont, California.

Author Dana Brookins goes all out for Halloween, more so than for any other holiday of the year. She gives and receives gifts as if it were Christmas, except the presents are all hobgoblinish. Last year after returning from an October trip to Missouri, where she had spent her childhood, and where she speaks annually at a children's library convention, she began to understand why she liked Halloween so much. Not only was the autumn gorgeous there, but the town went overboard decorating for Halloween. The autumnal celebration just might remind her of the past, of home, of roots.

But there's more at work than fond remembrances. Ritual, no matter how insignificant, is the glue that binds the pieces of our lives together.

The best rituals don't necessarily take place during the

major holidays. The healthiest are sometimes personal ones created by individuals. If a person alone performs a ritual that was once shared with family or friends, it helps put life in perspective.

Even working out at the gym can be a type of ritual. "People who work out have a sense of the right and wrong way to do things. Doing the routines gives them strength when things are under tension," says Brenneis.

Health experts believe celebrations and rituals are more important than ever. "Years ago, people didn't feel the same stress to plan out their lives in unfamiliar settings," says Walter Brackelmans, a Southern California psychiatrist. "If your father was a blacksmith, that's what you became. There were celebrations and rituals that took place, but they weren't as important as they are today because you already felt rooted. Rituals tend to represent, symbolically, a connectedness for family members. Through ritual we get a clear account of our own identity. When families or individuals are in trouble, one of the first things to go is the ritual celebration. The connecting structure is fractured."

Healthy singles don't wait to be asked to special holiday functions; they host them themselves. One psychologist who counsels single women says that many of them complain about not being asked to such special events such as Christmas or Thanksgiving dinners, but never would think of hosting the affair themselves and asking friends and relatives.

Barbara Cunningham recalls that when her kids were teens she used to get together with several other single mothers and rent a cabin in the mountains for Thanksgiving. It became a ritual and one she remembers fondly.

Glenna McAnish remembers the poverty she and her children lived in when she was a single mom. They sometimes ate popcorn for dinner. "We had nothing but we always made do," she says. Still, every year when Glenna got the income tax return they headed for the beach in Mexico. "It was the only reprieve we got," she says. "My kids still talk about that yearly trek to Mexico. It was a highlight of their lives. Do you think they would have remembered getting a new refrigerator?"

During this trip to Mexico, McAnish's children weren't allowed to call her "mom." In Mexico, they were no longer the "poor family on the block." McAnish wasn't mom. She was Glenna, the Irish Queen.

Attendance at functions like football games is considered by some health professionals a ritual that can release tension and give one a shared group experience, says Brenneis.

David Phillips, professor of sociology at the University of California at San Diego, says that deaths are in fact sometimes *postponed* until the person has reached an important occasion. This implies that psychological influences such as celebrations can prolong life.

One note of caution: Celebrations and rituals can be unhealthy when they become too rigid and demanding, but the experts agree that we should celebrate every chance we get because life is tough.

There are some celebrations—Christmas is an example—that are sometimes blown out of proportion. They end up making people feel worse instead of better.

Handling Holiday Guilt

A friend once asked if I knew how to make a pecan pie. She'd been invited to a holiday dinner with 18 snarling relatives and had been asked to bring this particular dessert.

"They called and asked me last week and I couldn't think of an excuse fast enough not to go," she complained. "Last year I had dinner with just my father and my own two children and it was lovely. How did I get into this?"

This is not a mean, Scrooge-like woman. She's simply among the many of us who belong to the Twinge-of-Guilt-Trip Holiday Club. We don't go places because we want to, but because we're supposed to. And nothing reinforces our should-do's like Christmas—the time of year reserved for the biggest guilt trip of all.

Through divorce and remarriages, many children now have four or more sets of grandparents, and trying to avoid hurt feelings is akin to running a marathon race with gunnysacks full of potatoes tied to your knees. One woman who shares custody of her two boys with her ex-husband is often greeted by relatives with, "Oh, poor thing. Your ex's turn this year?"

Why is this woman a poor thing? The truth is, she's lucky to have a former husband who loves his kids enough to want them on holidays. Kids have a way of picking up on how much they're loved and wanted. They need all the love and attention they can get.

Most of us are bullied into giving some explanation for the children's absence, however. That's what guilt does to us.

Guilt also forces people to host these occasions.

LONELINESS, DEPRESSION, AND OTHER NORMALITIES

My Aunt Bessie didn't enjoy hostess-playing, but the chore was foisted on her one year by a relative who intimated that it was her turn to make Thanksgiving dinner.

In her youth, Aunt Bessie had been the city kid who came to visit the rest of the family on the farm and refused to milk the cows or go swimming in the old swimmin' hole. She would rather buff her fingernails or sit under the peach tree reading. As an adult, she still didn't like to do things the rest of the family did. Still, she was finally forced to share her well-kept and tidy castle with 30 hungry, festive relatives.

Upon arriving and viewing the graciously spread table, Uncle Ned remarked, "Why, Bessie, you shouldn't have gone to all this trouble."

"You're damn right I shouldn't have," she replied, "and I'm never going to do it again," she replied.

Health professionals offer these tips to avoid the guilt trap:

- —Develop support systems where you can air your holiday guilt.
- —Don't think that getting together with the family is going to resolve past conflicts.
- —Get rid of the "shoulds" you believe are necessary for the holidays and instead, go for the "wants." The season can be fun if you're in control.
- —Do the things that will bring you into harmony with the environment and the season.
- —Develop more realistic expectations about the season.
- —Be certain to get exercise and don't abuse drugs, alcohol or food.
- —Take some responsibility for the holidays. Don't expect others to fill any void you might be feeling.

The holidays are no tougher for single people than for couples. All are hit with a variety of emotions during the holidays. Most of us have greater expectations of Christmas and Thanksgiving than are possible to fulfill, and that's part of the problem.

The worst-case scenario is a single woman sitting around bemoaning the fact that she wasn't invited anywhere for Christmas. What's to stop her from throwing her own party? What's to stop her from volunteering her Christmas Day at a soup kitchen set up for the homeless?

When it comes to the holidays, single people probably have more choices about what to do and what not to do than their married counterparts. We just have to sort out fact from fiction, and there's a lot of fiction surrounding the holidays.

Psychologist Marcia Lasswell says there are people who "by and large are dependent on others to make them feel better. They expect someone to call them and invite them someplace. Prior to holidays, I talk with people who feel sorry for themselves, and I ask them what they are cooking for dinner and who are they inviting."

Lois Langland, the never-married psychology professor, says that she invites others, including families, to her home during holidays. "I treat myself as a family," she says. "I've always been bothered when people invite you to their home because they want to make sure you're not alone on the holidays. I don't like the feeling that someone has to look out for you like you're some poor thing.

"There are women who will wait to be asked, but they haven't assumed an adult role yet. I think that one thing that makes a healthful single is that you're not apologetic."

Depression

Healthy single people don't become depressed any more often or more deeply than married women. Some studies show we may actually suffer less depression, but that's not to say we're entirely free of it.

"When I'm really in a down mood," says De Creasy, "I don't want to be with people. But if I'm at the point where I think I should do something about it, I make an effort to go out and be with people. I find out who's available to play. Still, there are definitely times when a person should just go to bed and pull the covers over her head," says Creasy.

About 80 percent of the population suffer some form of depression at one time or another—from mild blues to severe depressive disorders. Women are twice as likely to suffer from depression as men. Reasons range from hormones to the introspective way women look at the world. This latter tendency makes women more sensitive, but it also wreaks havoc with our psyches.

Depression can be a feeling of helplessness and hopelessness that doesn't go away, and which begins to interfere with a person's normal routine. However, depression needn't only be psychological. People who are aware that they are suffering chronic depression should consult a health professional because many physical conditions can cause depression including infections, cancer, head injuries, autoimmune diseases and diseases of the thyroid, adrenal or pituitary glands. Other causes include drugs such as steroids, birth control pills, hypertension medications and combinations of certain drugs.

Some depressions have a genetic basis, according to

Lewis L. Judd, M.D., former director of the National Institute of Mental Health. "An inherited tendency toward depression is the most powerful risk factor there is. That, combined with accumulated stress in the environment, is the basis for many depressive disorders."

Judd refers to the blues and short-term depressive states as a "transient disporic mood," and says reassuringly, "Everyone experiences those evanescent feelings that are part of the human condition. But they are distinctly different from clinically significant depression."

Recognizing that occasional depression is okay, and that if it's persistent, treatment doesn't mean eternal therapy, can, in itself, cast a hopeful new light on your feelings of sadness. Only a fool doesn't get depressed or blue once in a while. Sometimes all it takes is watching the nightly news.

Some research indicates that people with a mild depression see the world more realistically than those who never get depressed. This doesn't mean we can't put on rose-colored glasses to help us overcome the world's greyness once in a while. But neither is it a sin to occasionally loll in misery once in a while.

Some of the women interviewed for this book have indeed suffered depression—some requiring treatment. Others have had general or mild forms of depression.

But Wold says of depression: "Funny you should mention depression. I've just been going through a spell of it. I've just about decided allergies have much to do with it because my depression always seems so bad in September. I fight it for a long time—usually till I'm worn out and then I give in and wallow, really wallow in it. Then I decide I'm either going to climb out or die. So far, I've always climbed out."

Wold accepts her periods of depression as normal and says her mother and grandmother suffered the same type of angst.

"I remember my mother always sitting in a rocking chair reading a book," she says. "My grandmother read a lot too. I guess they just escaped through books. I always vowed I wouldn't be a person who just sat and read."

"I can fight it [depression] unless three factors come together: if my life isn't working out the way I think it should be and things seem to be getting too complicated, if something really major happens that creates a problem, and if my allergies and arthritis start acting up at the same time. Then I can't sleep and am tired all day and can't get my stuff done.

"When I feel like that, I don't want to be around anybody and don't want anybody around me. The way I usually cope is to get a good book, curl up in bed, buy a six-pack of beer and just wallow in being depressed until I'm so sick of it that I get out of bed and tell myself that I've gone as far with the wallowing as is possible."

Elizabeth Bacon says that once in a while she decides she's had enough and takes to her bed for an entire day of eating chocolate bars and watching videos.

As singles we sometimes start thinking that our being single has something to do with our depression. In fact the angst is within us. Women who look for a man to ease their depression often find nothing more than grief. They're the only ones responsible for their happiness or down times—and besides, married women also have periods of depression.

Another misconception is that women suffer more depression during menopause. Research at the University of Alabama at Birmingham *did* find that about 20 percent of the women in a study believed they are "supposed" to be depressed during the menopausal stage of their lives.

One fiftyish woman I know who had been feeling tired and mildly depressed went to her doctor and was told, "Well, it could just be your age. You know . . . menopause." She snapped at the doctor: "Don't tell a woman that. That's a cop-out. I came to you for help, not some tired old platitude."

Some researchers think depression may affect the body to such an extent that it causes irregular heart rhythms or aggravates the progression of arteriosclerosis. Depression might adversely affect motivation, which leads to a breakdown of normal routines, including the exercise necessary to keep the body healthy, says Robert Carney, associate professor of psychology at Washington University in St. Louis, Missouri.

Depression doesn't have to mean endless days of losing work, sleep and friends. If you're in a rut and feel you can't get out of it, seek the help of a professional.

VIII

Tips and Tricks to Staying Healthy

"All the social science literature is coming to view the healthy person as one who has "self" control (control of her own life), self-direction, and autonomy."
—Janet Giele, sociologist, Brandeis University

Mind over Matter

Women who choose to live alone are very conscious of health. We know that if we get sick, no one is going to be around to baby us. This doesn't mean we're invincible. We simply know that when we're down and out, our goal is to get going again, which may be easier for us because the type of person who goes against the social imperative to marry and who makes no apologies for it is often hardy to begin with.

The key to this hardiness is, as Janet Giele calls it, "self" control. Estelle Ramey, the noted endocrinologist, has found evidence of the power of "self" control in studies she's done on stress.

When we hear the phrase "killer stress," we usually think of the workaholic or the hard-running executive or the typical rat-race competitor. But in fact the most noxious life-threatening stress is the perception of lack of control, and that's even true for rats.

"You take rats and put them in a negative-positive reinforcement—food for the right action and electric shock for the wrong, and in this situation the rats learn real fast," says Ramey. "The rats can go on with this experiment for months and only the experimenter will feel stress.

"Then you change the signals, as they are often changed for married women," Ramey goes on. "These women have learned all the rules of the game. They're married, have children, and are great wives and mothers. Then hubby comes home and says he has nothing against her, but he needs someone closer to his own age—like 18. In other words, these women have been switched to new rules. They have no 'self' control. When this is done to rats, they bleed internally and die.

"Single women have been playing by these same rules. A woman who has defied society's expectations may run into trouble, but she's still in control of her life as much as anyone can be," says Ramey. "The rules haven't been changed on her because she never played the game to begin with."

Another study on how "self" control affects health was done on men and women, both married and single, who were listed in *Who's Who in America*. As Ramey points out, "Anyone listed in *Who's Who* is an achiever and workaholic. And they can't survive that kind of life unless they are strong to begin with.

"But these high achievers don't have stress problems. Studies show that top managers seem to have fewer health problems than middle managers who don't have as much control over their situation."

Ramey says that when women entered the work force in great numbers and took on demanding jobs, health experts (mostly men) expected them to suffer the same job-related stress problems men did. "But they didn't," she says. "It was just wishful thinking that they would."

What working outside the home did for these women, whether married or single, was provide them with more control over their own lives, which reduces stress.

Ramey, herself married and a grandmother, is nearing 80. She believes that in the future women will have even more "self" control, and therefore longer lives, because they are going to college and developing economic bases prior to marriage. Not surprisingly, a recent German study showed that when executive women quit their positions to have children, their levels of HDL, the good cholesterol, went down and the levels of LDL, the bad cholesterol, increased.

"When I lecture, I always ask my audiences, 'If you were being driven someplace in a blinding snowstorm, who do you think would have the higher level of stress—you or the driver?' Of course the passenger has higher levels of stress because that person doesn't have control of the situation. It's in someone else's hands," she says.

Sometimes when you seem to lose control of your life, even momentarily, you can feel illness creeping in. You might even begin to doubt yourself. I've done it.

One occurrence was soon after my father died. I was trying to place my mother, who has Alzheimer's, in a nursing facility; tend to his funeral arrangements; take care of their business; and handle a myriad of other things. I drove home late one night in winter snow to my home in the mountains. The house was cold and so was the bed. I'd been having headaches and overeating, had a runny nose, and just generally didn't feel good. As I crawled into bed I had the fleeting thought, "I wish I had a man to help me through some of this."

But that thought was quickly replaced with, "No, because in addition to taking care of my folks' business, attending to the funeral, getting mama placed, and keeping up with my own job, I'd have to take care of a man too."

It isn't that single women are blessed with an unequal share of good health. They might, however, react differently to illness from how a married woman would react, because they have no one to whom they can complain.

Dorothy Macy, the woman who has lived single since 1947 when her husband, a government scientist, was killed in an accident, has had to slow down this past year because she injured her knee working in the garden. She resents the inconvenience.

"I've never been super-healthy," she says. "I've had gall bladder surgery, an ulcer, diverticulitis—but when you're single and alone, you're very conscious of taking care of yourself. You do watch it a little closer because you want to stay independent as long as possible."

Lucky are those who stay healthy into and through old age, but not everyone is so blessed. Single women worry about being alone and aging. Because we have developed independent natures, many of us fear not being able to take care of ourselves. Yet the majority of married women are going to become widows simply because women outlive men. Being married is no guarantee that someone is going to be around when a woman gets sick.

My mother, now 75, was a strong, healthy woman who kept her mind stimulated. Still, she's in a nursing facility now suffering from Alzheimer's. We may have control of our own lives, which in turn may help lower stress-related illnesses, but some things happen in which we have no choice. We can try to will away illness. We can be New Age gurus. But when certain cells, possibly programmed by our genes, decide it's time to malfunction, as in the case of diseases like Alzheimer's and Parkinson's, our health status is out of our hands.

Macy's secret to feeling healthy and overcoming her illnesses is keeping busy most of the time. She kept herself occupied by raising a daughter by herself, working full-time, taking care of aging parents, traveling, belonging to a variety of clubs and cooking. "I like to cook," she says, "but I don't like housework or crafts."

Women who choose to be single aren't necessarily health nuts or exercise buffs. They each have their own little tricks to staying healthy, though. Whether our particular health regimens work or not if put to scientific testing is moot. If drinking herbal tea or taking certain vitamins or consulting the Tarot cards makes a person feel physically or mentally healthier, then that's her personal business. Some work out at gyms, play tennis, jog, speed-walk or use an exercise bike at home. Others do none of the above. All, however, are aware that physical well-being contributes to the self-esteem that is necessary for singlehood. A flexible attitude probably has a great impact on how we feel. Artist Stormy Sandquist says, "I've always eaten a diet balanced between good food and junk food. I've eaten so much junk food that I'm well-preserved. I do eat lots of veggies, but I get pretty crotchety if I don't have a sticky gooey bun with my morning coffee."

There are steps we can take for overall better health or to give us a boost during times of stress. The following tips came from some of the single women I've interviewed.

Seven Health-Boosters for Tip-Top Shape

In addition to taking "self" control, not smoking, lowering LDL or raising HDL cholesterol levels, getting proper nutrition, exercise and the right amount of sleep, there are other health-boosters which will add to the quality of life. They don't require special equipment, additional time or trips to the doctor's. Nor do they require that you give anything up. They're free. All they do is add quality and the possibility of adding a few more years to a person's life.

1. Plan leisure time.

A growing number of health professionals say that people who know how to enjoy their leisure enhance every aspect of their lives, including health. Unfortunately, too many people stumble helter-skelter into what they consider leisure instead of planning ahead for fun and games. Although people sense that leisure is good for them, most don't know exactly what it is.

Until 10 or 15 years ago, leisure was defined almost by default. "Whatever time was left over after working, cooking, and taking care of children, was considered leisure," says Howard E. Tinsley, professor of psychology at Southern Illinois University at Carbondale. Because health professionals know that leisure is vital to health, Tinsley believes today's definitions should include (1) freedom of choice, (2) intrinsic motivations, (3) a sense of stimulation, and (4) a sense of commitment or investment.

People who spend more time in leisure activities have higher degrees of life-satisfaction and are physically and mentally healthier than those who don't plan for leisure activity. "The trick is finding out your own special leisure-nook, though," says Tinsley.

Betty Wold, who turned 70 in 1991, talks about grabbing an innertube and a beer at the end of a summer day and heading for the river with friends. Because she runs an herb farm, she is able to incorporate business with pleasure by traveling to herbal conferences and festivals.

Wold works hard but she believes it's important for single women to pamper themselves. "Set a nice table just for you," she advises. "My table now is loaded with a broken scarf clip, two pens, magazines, purse, jacket, tapes, papers, pictures, a tape recorder and herb labels. It's all stuff accumulated today and haven't had time to do anything with. So I will fix a plate and dine on the front porch. It's important to have one place that is neat so I can ignore all the rest of it. I can go to that one corner [on the porch] and nothing yammers 'Clean me up.'"

Thomas B. Holman, associate professor of family science at Brigham Young University, Utah, agrees with Wold. "Ideally," he says, "leisure is time to get away from the routines of the day."

The English novelist George Eliot wrote: "Leisure is gone; gone where the spinning-wheels are gone, and the pack horses, and the slow wagons, and the peddlers who brought bargains to the door on sunny afternoons." Eliot was right. And so we must accommodate to the changes in society. Many of the singles I spoke with said that never in their lifetimes will they be able to do all the things they want to do.

For some, puttering around in the yard or making household repairs falls under leisure-time activities. For others, home maintenance is pure torture. Each of us has to determine what constitutes leisure to us. Developing your own leisure time means finding out what turns you on. "We need to develop our own melody, our own area that we get joy and pleasure from," says noted oncologist Carl Simonton, a pioneer in the philosophy of developing a playful way of life.

2. Develop support groups.

Psychologist Martin Barry Schlosser of the Clarity Consulting Corporation in Westport, Connecticut, says that what researchers call "hardy women," those who seem to have fewer illnesses and who bounce back fast from adversity, seem to have a knack for developing good relationships. When they have a problem, they might share it, but they seldom dump emotional baggage on friends. They know the value of friendships and make conscious efforts to keep them alive.

Although many studies have indicated that women are more adept than men at developing close relationships, new research at the University of Southern California by Gerald P. Jones says it appears that males whose self-concept incorporates some positive elements of the traditional female role are also capable of these close friendships.

3. Volunteer time.

Nearly 50 percent of the adult population volunteers time for such causes as working with the homeless, the illiterate, the abused, and raising funds for everything from cancer research to saving the whales. The time Americans report volunteering has increased 35 percent in the past five years.

Although the reason for volunteering may be altruism, the result may be a strong immune system, increased life expectancy and vitality, and reduced stress.

Research psychologist Jerry Lee at Loma Linda University Medical Center in California, says that people who do volunteer work live longer and healthier lives than those who don't. "If I were a practicing psychologist," he says, "I'd tell my clients to get out and work as volunteers."

At a 1989 conference in New York at the Institute for the Advancement of Health, it was suggested that people who help others, reduce their own feelings of helplessness and depression because of an increased sense of self-worth.

The late physician Hans Selye, who is credited with founding modern stress research, maintained that when people do good it inspires gratitude and affection from others, and this warmth protects the do-gooders from the stresses of life.

His belief is supported by the research of Irene M. Thorelli of the University of Wisconsin-La Crosse. Her studies show that volunteers want much more affection from others than do typical citizens, and that they get it from their volunteer work. Wanting and needing this affection may be healthier than ever before suspected.

Rebecca Kuzins, a single and a journalist in her 30s, says that her volunteer work with a literacy program gave her more pleasure than her job as a reporter.

Ruth Dever, 80, began tutoring two years ago in a local literacy program sponsored by a nearby library. She feels it's a high point of her life. The first man she tutored was an unemployed alcoholic who could neither read nor write. He's now functioning at high school level, plans to go to college, has quit drinking, and is interested in politics.

Dever was asked to head the literacy program and accept a salary, but she refused the offer. "I get too much pleasure out of what I'm doing to turn it into a job," she said.

4. Keep a household pet.

C. Edward Koop, M.D., former surgeon general of the United States, said that pets can sometimes benefit the mental and physical welfare of disabled persons better than any medicine or doctor. Many nursing homes now promote visitation by pets. Inconclusive research indicates that owning pets promotes health, and that pet owners tend to live longer than those who have no pets.

Therapist-physiologist Elizabeth Corson of Columbus, Ohio, and her husband, Samuel Corson, M.D., are experts on human-pet interaction. They say that cats in particular can give many old people reasons for living, and that when people feel down, taking care of an animal makes them feel strong and nurturing. "They can feel on top of things," says Elizabeth Corson. "Pets are nonjudgmental. They accept people with all their flaws."

Corson warns that research promising longer lives for people who own pets might be misleading. "It could be that people who choose to live with and take care of pets have the types of personalities that help them live longer," she says. "In some cases pets aren't good for people—if the people have allergies, if the pets are troublesome, if they cause problems between family members. But under the right circumstances, pets are definitely healthful."

Nearly all the single women I've interviewed own pets. Sometimes they complain about having to provide for them when they go on vacation, or what nuisances they can be, but none of them would give up their pets. As one woman said, "When I come home at night, there's my dog wagging his tail. It's nice to have someone there, but he also allows me to do some nurturing of my own."

When we talk to our pets, our blood pressure goes down. When we talk to humans, it goes up. This happens because talking to dogs, cats, birds, and even fish, is much less stressful than talking to people, according to Aaron Katcher, associate professor of psychiatry at the University of Pennsylvania Center for the Interaction of Animals and Society.

"It's touch-talk dialogue. Touching pets is affectionate dialogue," he says, adding that more than 80 percent of pet owners say they talk to their charges as if the pets were human. Some even tell personal secrets to their animals.

5. Wear rose-colored glasses.

Those called "hardy people" by researchers tend to wear rose-colored glasses, and that's okay, according to a growing number of mental health experts. Martin Barry Schlosser says that having a Pollyanna world view—that is, not feeling threatened by the world—is a healthy attitude.

His views are in keeping with a growing number of mental health professionals who believe that a little self-deception is healthy. Shelley Taylor, professor of psychology at the University of California at Los Angeles and author of *Positive Illusions*, says that people draw strength from positive illusions or deceptions. "People who have a sense of control over stressful events show a lower neuroendocrine response to stress," says Taylor.

These new studies are causing the mental health community to re-evaluate old beliefs about the need to confront stark realities.

Another deception is to "keep some of it in" rather than

letting it all hang out. Eric Eisenberg, an assistant professor of communication arts and sciences at the University of Southern California, says that when people disclose all their feelings and opinions, they alienate friends, colleagues and family members.

In other words, a bit of deception is good for your health, if it means wearing rose-colored glasses sometimes and not always bombarding people with your honest opinion.

Glenna McAnish has her own strategy for self-deception. "I've been blessed with a supremely positive attitude," she says. In our family is a house leprechaun called Timothy. I always told my children about Timothy and about the little folk; I think maybe Timothy and God were rolled into one. I remember a time when my girls were three and four years old and we didn't have any money. I found a $20 bill in the mailbox. No envelope or anything. The kids asked where it came from and I said, 'Probably Timothy.'

"I think my life has been richer because I haven't been married and I've learned to rely on myself and on Timothy. I've seen to it that my life is filled with richness. When I was married, I expected my husband to fill my life with those riches and it didn't happen. I have a wonderful life and I'm not lonely. I have 'affectionate' male friendships, but haven't been interested in remarrying."

6. Be assertive, not angry.

Blowing off steam might be good for Mount St. Helens in Washington State, but it's not all that good for people. According to current medical thought, how people handle their anger may make the difference between health and distress.

For years experts said it was best to vent anger, to the point of hitting one another with soft objects to prevent turning that venom into ulcers or heart attacks. New research indicates that holding in anger doesn't cause ulcers, heart attacks or depression. Holding the anger long enough to think about it, and then reacting, may be the best reaction.

Used this way, anger can be productive. Not that you have to become a wimp, but waiting simply gives you time to think of something constructive to do with the anger.

Vincent L. DeQuattro, M.D., of the University of Southern California School of Medicine, reports that reduced levels of anger and hostile thoughts are linked with lower blood pressure.

Psychologist Robert Ellis, author of *Anger: How to Live With and Without It*, says we need to accept the fact that we create our own anger. Another person may be doing something that smacks of stupidity or rottenness, but we can choose how to react to the incident.

Some health professionals say people should just try counting to ten when they get angry. But many of the single women I've interviewed said that the best way to handle anger is to try to do something about the situation that caused the anger, whether the effort is successful or not.

Examples: If you feel slighted by someone, ask for an explanation rather than letting the wound fester. If you believe you've been cheated on a mechanic's bill, complain to the mechanic, and if that doesn't work, contact your local consumer's protection agency.

Dana Brookins had a long-time friend, once a neighbor, who lived in a distant city. They had kept in touch by mail and with occasional visits. At one point Brookins began to feel that her longtime friend was neglecting the relationship, so she wrote and aired her feelings. Within two months the friend had arranged to visit. She apologized for getting so caught up in her work that she had neglected equally important aspects of her life.

Once I was given a ticket for doing 80 miles per hour in a 55 zone. I was actually pushing 65 at the time, but the officer said he had the higher speed on radar. I know nothing of radar, but I knew my 4-cylinder Suburu wouldn't go 80 up an incline, which was where I'd been stopped. I asked friends about fighting the ticket and they said to forget it, that I couldn't beat radar. But I decided to fight it. If I lost, at least I'd have had my day in court. I did have my day in court, paid a reduced fine reflecting a lowered speed, and walked out feeling better than if I had simply paid the ticket to begin with. I did what I had to do and then was ready to get on with my life.

Airing grievances is important to well-being. Studies in the workplace have shown that stress isn't the biggest threat to health; not having any control over the situation *is*. Not being able to vent your frustrations to a boss creates more stress than overwork. This is true of life in general.

Ramey believes that women handle anger better than men because women can cry about it. She recalls a professor who came into her office complaining about a parking space that had been taken away from him. "He was shouting and I asked him not to yell," she says. "I told him it was bad for my auditory system. I asked him to cry instead. Violent rage is seen as good in men, but they aren't allowed to cry. Women are allowed to cry but not to pound the desk. Tears are a safer way of dealing with interpersonal problems. No one has ever been killed because of crying, but they have been killed because of unrestrained rage. Unfortunately, men are supposed to cry only when their mother dies or when a certain football team wins."

7. Learn to forgive.
Forgiveness is another tool for overcoming anger, but most people need to learn how, says psychiatrist Richard P. Fitzgibbons, M.D., of Bala Cynwyd, Pennsylvania.

Fitzgibbons, an expert on forgiveness, believes it's the only way to truly resolve anger and conflicts. He defines forgiveness as "the surrender of one's desire for revenge."

"By forgiveness, I don't mean just praying about it," he says. People can learn to let go of their anger through forgiveness by first doing it intellectually. They should ask themselves, "Do I harbor anger against So-and-so?" Then they can try to understand what made So-and-so act that way, and then let go of it.

Most people don't deal with anger from their childhoods, he says, so they marry and bring this baggage with them. When they become angry at their partners, the first thing they have to do is ask themselves if they have failed to resolve old anger that might be spilling into present relationships. This unconscious anger is a major form of stress, and can affect not only relationships but physical health as well.

"Resolving anger takes time," says Fitzgibbons. "It is a process. But in the long run it's better than denying anger, and it's certainly better than expressing anger. I have a theory that people can't learn to express anger anyway, until they have learned how to forgive. It's only then that the pool of unconscious anger diminishes and they can deal with existing anger in an appropriate manner."

When Betty Wold was going through a divorce in her 50s, she was saturated with anger. Fortunately, she has a great sense of humor. She was a teacher, and for the last day of school she baked a cake to share with the staff. It was a wedding cake, replete with plastic bride and bridegroom on the top, except the bridegroom was turned upside-down with his head stuck in the icing. After the party, Wold got on with the rest of her life. She had done something about her anger, so she was able to forgive.

8. Add laughter to your life.

Long before any scientific research on laughter, human beings suspected that a good belly laugh had curative powers. "Early physicians used to tell jokes to their patients and laugh with them," says immunologist Lee S. Berk of Loma Linda University School of Medicine.

God forbid that we should be afraid to let out a good laugh because we fear laugh lines. I remember a television talk-show hosted by an aging beauty who had maintained her looks quite well. She said she never smiled enough to cause creases. What a sad way to try to be beautiful. I'll bet she didn't know how good laughter is for health, and health is where true beauty lies.

Laughter appears to help the body prevent or fight illness by boosting the immune system through changes in white blood cell counts and certain hormones, says Berk. Additionally, a good belly laugh is akin to jogging because it increases the heart rate, speeds breathing, raises the blood pressure and increases oxygen consumption. Afterwards, breathing and heart rates slow, usually below normal levels, the blood pressure drops and muscles relax.

William Fry, M.D., professor of clinical psychiatry at Stanford University Medical Center, says that laughing

100 times a day is equivalent to 10 minutes of rowing exercise.

Hospitals across the nation are installing laughter rooms where they show funny movies, or providing television comedy channels to keep patients laughing. At DeKalb General Hospital in Decatur, Georgia, patients who seem close to giving up are given a prescription for a few hours in a humor room. "The doctor will write it out just like a regular medication order," says Sandra Yates, a head nurse.

When you're feeling real alone, blue or even sick, a good idea is to rent some comedy videos and spend a few evenings watching them.

Protecting Your Cardiovascular System

One area of health that threatens everyone, but is frequently denied by women, is the heart attack. To many of us the words "heart attack" inspire an image of a middle-aged man lying in a hospital bed, hooked up to an intravenous feeder with a nervous wife standing nearby. That vision is a myth.

Heart attack is only one of several diseases affecting the heart and blood vessels. Cardiovascular disease is the number-one killer of women over 40, outranking cancer by more than two to one. So why do women give short shrift to a disease that eventually kills 50 percent of us?

For one thing, heart attacks don't affect women at the early age they do men. Women's hormones protect them, and their blood vessels are more elastic than men's (for protection during pregnancy), so when the blood rushes through our bodies, the vessels give a little. Not in men.

Once women are past menopause, the special protection ends, but still we don't give cardiovascular disease much thought.

Clearly, this intricate blood processing system that suffers from the effects of high cholesterol diets, smoking, sedentary lifestyles and stress isn't just the domain of men. Unfortunately, most cardiovascular research in the past has centered on men. Even when women have been included in newer studies, their reactions, prognoses and treatments are evaluated and compared to those of men, says Margaret A. Chesney, associate adjunct professor in the department of epidemiology and biostatistics at the University of California School of Medicine in San Francisco.

Researchers are recognizing these differences and designing separate studies that eliminate the female/male comparisons. Women themselves are demanding that their personal health practitioners take note of these cardiovascular differences between men and women because some of them make women more vulnerable to heart disease.

We women have some plusses going for us. Our blood vessels are more resilient to the onslaught of cholesterol and fats, although this protection doesn't last forever unless we develop healthy habits early on. But women's reaction to various forms of cardiovascular disease is made more complicated because of smaller body, heart and vessel size; the disease is usually diagnosed later in life; current diagnostic tools aren't as effective on women; women have higher mortality rates once stricken; they have a poorer response to heart bypass and angioplasty; and they don't respond as well to some of the current therapies.

When women suffer from, say, coronary heart disease,

they often fail to take heed because it masks itself as chest pain, which they might brush off as indigestion. When men have coronary heart disease, they often suffer a severe heart attack as a first symptom and are treated immediately and extensively. We women march on believing we're tougher than our male counterparts because our life spans are generally longer, so we shove cardiovascular fitness into the background of our lives. Eventually it may catch up with us at about age 40 or thereabouts and we're hit with the big bang of cardiovascular disease.

Even so, women continue to shrug off the possibility of cardiovascular disease. Most of us believe that cancer is our number-one killer, when in actuality about 500,000 women die annually of cardiovascular diseases, compared to about 220,000 for cancer. When a woman suffers a heart attack, she's twice as likely as a man to die from it within the first two weeks.

Despite these gloomy statistics, the mortality rates for cardiovascular disease have declined by 37 percent in the past seven years. Myron L. Weisfeldt, M.D., president of the American Heart Association, attributes much of this decline to healthier lifestyles, advances in medical diagnosis and treatment, and an increasing awareness of the problem.

Weisfeldt agrees with other health professionals that most women haven't adopted healthier lifestyles just to accommodate their fear of cardiovascular disease. It's more likely that as women have taken on more responsibility for making the world go round they've found these healthy lifestyle changes give them more energy to get the job done. They're also more aware that diet has something to do with cancer, as does stress.

"The fallout is . . . women have inadvertently been protecting their cardiovascular systems," Weisfeldt says. But they can do even better if they acknowledge that at certain stages of their lives they're more vulnerable than men to this disease. In doing so, they can not only lower the high incidence of cardiovascular disease, but improve the quality of their lives.

The lifestyle changes that affect cardiovascular fitness, and that improve the quality of life for nearly everyone, include abstaining from smoking cigarettes; limiting alcohol consumption; exercising; reducing stress; staying within weight guidelines; reducing total fat and cholesterol intake; and meeting the daily needs for protein, vitamins, minerals and other nutrients.

Although natural aging and hereditary factors can't be changed, the following preventable risk factors outweigh in importance the unchangeable ones:

Smoking. Women who smoke are at a two to six times greater risk of developing cardiovascular disease than those who don't smoke. If a woman smokes and takes the contraceptive pill, she's 30 times more likely to develop cardiovascular disease. Although statistics show a drop in smoking overall, the use of cigarettes is still rising among young women.

High blood pressure. Although hypertension has a hereditary connection, and nearly half of all women over 55 have high blood pressure, the condition can be controlled and treated effectively with lifestyle changes and/or medication. Women with hereditary hypertension usually must resort to medications. Most women, however, can control high blood pressure with a healthier lifestyle. There are a few programs in the country that check for hypertension in school-age children. When the condition is detected early on, significant and permanent lifestyle changes can prevent later problems.

High levels of cholesterol. There may also be hereditary factors in cholesterol levels, but all the evidence isn't in. Until about age 45, women tend to have lower cholesterol levels than men. Even when the levels rise, women still tend to have more HDLs (high-density lipoproteins) that help flush out the bad LDLs (low-density lipoproteins). So, all in all, women can handle higher levels of cholesterol better than men because of their advantageous HDL levels.

It is believed that HDLs carry cholesterol out of the arteries to the liver where it is eliminated from the body, and that LDLs tend to stay in the body and build up in the artery walls.

Still, approximately one-third of all American women have dangerously high levels of cholesterol, putting them at high risk of developing cardiovascular disease. Women need to have cholesterol checked routinely, especially if levels approach those considered unsafe: above 200 mg/dl (milligrams per deciliter).

High triglycerides. Women can't tolerate those fatty acids in the blood called triglycerides as well as men. The higher their triglyceride levels, the greater the risk of heart attack. Triglyceride is the chemical form in which most fats exist. High triglyceride levels often accompany higher total cholesterol and LDL cholesterol levels and a lower HDL cholesterol level. High triglycerides are also related to the risk of developing diabetes, another risk factor for heart disease.

Scientists haven't confirmed that high triglycerides are an independent risk factor for cardiovascular disease, but one major study found that higher triglyceride levels are directly related to a higher risk of heart attack in women, though not in men. The reasons aren't yet clear and more research is being done. Triglyceride levels vary according to age and sex, but many doctors consider 85 to 250 mg/dl as normal.

Obesity. A person who is more than 20 percent above desirable weight is at greater risk of cardiovascular disease. One of the latest findings, which should please vast numbers of women, is that the weight they've accumulated through the years about the hips and thighs is healthier than the spare tires men tend to acquire around the middle. Weight gained around the middle is associated with a greater risk of heart disease in both men and women.

When other lifestyle changes are made, such as a reduction in fats and cholesterol intake, or an increase in exercise, weight loss becomes easier.

Diabetes. Approximately 70 percent of diabetics die of some form of cardiovascular disease, so diabetics should be monitored regularly by a physician.

Stress. Stress is a major risk factor that can be changed, although studies still aren't conclusive about its impact on cardiovascular disease. Research does suggest that hard-driving, type-A personalities who are also hostile, whether they be male or female, increase their risk of heart and artery diseases. Very recent studies show that simply being competitive, even a workaholic, won't in itself cause cardiovascular disease.

A highly recommended way to alleviate stress is for a woman to take more control over her life. The Framingham Heart Studies showed that women working as low-level clerks had a greater risk of heart attacks than did career women, because the career women had more control over their jobs.

Other studies show that higher education reduces the risk of cardiovascular disease. It appears that the highly educated adopt healthier lifestyle habits.

On the other hand, research from the University of Stockholm suggests that the multiple roles adopted by women who work and maintain family households contribute to stress. Unlike men, women are generally unable to unwind when they get home because of household and family duties. Biostatistician Margaret Chesney says that other studies show that even when men share tasks at home, women assume more responsibility for seeing that the tasks are done. Women judge themselves more harshly at work and at home, which frequently leads them to adverse health behavior such as smoking, overeating, loss of sleep, and alcohol consumption.

Estrogen replacement therapy (ERT). During childbearing years, the hormone estrogen seems to protect women from heart disease, while the same hormone increases the risk in men. Many studies have shown that as women age and estrogen diminishes, replacement therapy can make up for the lost estrogen. But estrogen replacement therapy (ERT) remains controversial because it appears to increase the risk of breast cancer.

Some health professionals believe that the benefits of ERT far outweigh the risk, especially now that doses have been lowered and are combined with progestin, a synthetic form of the hormone progesterone, to reduce whatever risk of uterine or breast cancer is associated with ERT. But progestin appears to diminish the beneficial effects estrogen has on the heart. Many scientists believe that the hormone-like fatty acid prostaglandin also plays a role in protecting women from heart disease, and research is ongoing in this area.

Dozens of studies in the United States and Canada over the past 10 years have shown that women who undergo ERT have one-third to one-half the risk of death from cardiovascular disease compared to women the same age who don't take the hormone. On the other hand, Meier J. Stampfer, M.D., assistant professor of medicine at Harvard Medical School, says that protection doesn't last long after ERT is discontinued.

Researcher Peter Wilson, M.D., director of laboratories for the Framingham Heart Studies in Massachusetts, says early studies begun in the 1960s indicated high cancer risks for women who used ERT. But the women in those earlier tests were given much larger doses of estrogen than are prescribed today, and many of the test subjects smoked.

In the meantime, scientists have drawn several conclusions about the effects of ERT. On the plus side: (1) estrogen replacement therapy may be beneficial in protecting postmenopausal women against heart disease; (2) when combined with progestin, ERT might provide added protection against endometrial cancer; (3) both hormones are prescribed in much lower doses than they were previously (the higher doses are believed to have caused ERT's negative side effects); (4) ERT helps protect against osteoporosis.

On the minus side: (1) women with a family history of uterine or breast cancer are at high risk of developing cancer with the use of ERT; (2) the addition of progestin may cancel out the benefits that estrogen provides for lowering cholesterol levels; (3) replacement estrogen may not cause breast cancer, but it might fuel the growth of pre-existing breast tumors; (4) in combination with smoking, ERT can be deadly.

Myron Weisfeldt, president of the American Heart Association, says that the latest studies increasingly point to dangers with ERT use. Along with many health practitioners, he believes that if a woman has a family history of breast cancer, she shouldn't take ERT, but if she has a family history of stroke among women in their 50s, ERT is probably a good idea.

Researcher Peter Wilson, like Weisfeldt, recommends that women and their physicians monitor closely the estrogen replacement, that the dose be kept as low as possible, and that ERT patients be warned against smoking.

Oral contraceptives. Birth control pills are another matter. Women who use oral contraceptives have at least three or four times the heart attack risk of women who don't. When birth control pills are combined with cigarettes, the risk rises even more dramatically. It is believed that oral contraceptives increase the danger of heart attack and stroke because they elevate blood cholesterol, blood pressure and blood sugar. For women already suffering cardiovascular disease the pill may contribute to the formation of blood clots.

But again, the studies on birth control pills, like those on ERT, were done years ago, when much higher doses of estrogen were used. More recent studies suggest that the newer lower doses of estrogen in birth control pills reduce this risk, but do not entirely eliminate it. Each woman has to make her own decision about the use of birth control pills based on her risk factors and on an evaluation by her health practitioner.

Although many preventive measures, such as the use of

ERT, remain unproven, it is clearly evident that women can lessen their risk of cardiovascular disease. As women adopt healthy lifestyle changes, they not only lower their risk of developing cardiovascular disease, they increase their chances of survival of other debilitating diseases.

Bouncing Back from Pain and Strain

We admire people who are resilient despite physical and psychological hardships, and we wonder what keeps them bouncing back. Physicians and mental health professionals are curious too. Many women who choose to be single are the type who bounce back. They seem to have been born with this toughness, and research indicates that some people do come equipped with nervous systems capable of withstanding large amounts of physical and psychic pain. Some appear to have psychological makeups that propel them onward no matter what.

Showing an emotional response to pain has a cultural basis. For some the sharing of feelings has a healing effect. For others, such a display may be socially unacceptable, and may even aggravate the pain.

Handling pain, mental or physical, is also linked to the person's view of life. "We could spill hot coffee on ten different people and we'd get ten different reactions," says Martin Barry Schlosser. "Later in the day, some will have forgotten the incident, but those who are still fuming tend to do the same thing with other stresses in their lives."

Whatever the cause of pain and the way it's handled remains "fairly mysterious," says Murray Wexler, M.D., professor of psychiatry and behavioral sciences, and a specialist in the psychological aspects of pain at the University of Southern California.

A person can learn to deal with pain more effectively through physical and psychological therapy. Then there are chemical painkillers, which are also often necessary, but pain relief is never a simple process.

"The fact is, we know of nothing that can eliminate pain," says Wexler. Conversely, he admits, "sometimes we'll treat someone who has been in constant pain for 15 years and it suddenly evaporates."

It's never simply physical pain the person has to deal with, even if they've been diagnosed with, say, a severe back problem. Psychological outlook also enters the picture. Coping with pain is a combination of the person's believing he or she has the resources to handle the pain, and then acting on it, according to Laurence Grimm, clinical psychologist and professor at the University of Illinois, Chicago. In the face of pain, "a person's problem-solving skills become very important," he says. "A lot depends on what they learned growing up."

Some have learned to roll with the punches and minimize the situation. Usually, this attitude is learned behavior, partially stemming from how their parents reacted to stress and pain. Or they may have also picked it up from peers. If siblings acted tough in the face of adversity, the person may have learned it from them.

Others have absorbed what Grimm calls catastrophic thinking. Their perception gets distorted and when something happens their minds race with thoughts such as, "Oh my God. What is the worst that can happen?" This attitude aggravates their reaction to pain or stress.

Grimm believes that too many people think of stress as

a reaction to external events. "They think they can rate the stress in a situation such as getting married or divorced, having a child, losing a job," he says. "But the truth is, people vary in what is perceived as a stressful event. To some, divorce might not be stressful at all."

On the other hand, being a stoic isn't always the answer if it leads to isolation during stressful periods.

"If a man loses his job, but is surrounded by a loving wife and family and friends, his reaction to stress will be less than a man who doesn't have that support," says Grimm. "If he loses the role of the provider, he has other roles, as a father, husband and friend."

Unfortunately, people who don't bounce back tend to let friendship fall by the wayside. They become engulfed in their pain and it emerges as the focal point of their lives. If you ask, "How's your day today?" they'll answer in terms of how their pain feels.

"Too often a person with chronic pain will become a social isolate," says Wexler. "We try to get them in tune with their environment and social activities again."

Finding social support can be difficult because some people have never learned how to make friends. "They were either rejected by their peers because they're obnoxious, or they just don't know how," says Grimm. "They stay relatively isolated and they go through stressful periods on their own. We can convince them they need social support, but then we have to teach them how to get it."

People who bounce back readily may also have physiological characteristics that make them tougher. Some people are born with cardiovascular systems that make them more responsive to stressful stimuli. And some people are born with a predisposition to develop psychosomatic disorders.

"The nervous system works in fairly complex ways, but one theory is that there is a sort of gate in the spinal system and under certain conditions more pain information gets through to the brain. Sometimes the gate is locked and the pain information doesn't get through," says Wexler.

"Perhaps if people are depressed, or have long histories of being hurt, punished or made to feel guilty, the gate is unlocked and more pain information comes through to the brain. Or there may be chemical factors involved in the opening or closing of the gate."

Another theory is that the nerve tracks are damaged by past pain experiences both physical and psychological, so a pattern is interpreted in the brain as pain, whether it is or not. Wexler likens it to having a personal credit card that an individual puts into the teller window. It gives a certain message that elicits a response. In the case of pain, the card carries inherited qualities, environmental characteristics (such as the way in which a person is raised), existing social support systems and a particular world view.

Pat Allen, a psychotherapist in Newport Beach, California, believes that people who seem to bounce back from adversity more readily than others have experienced many traumas in their lives, particularly in childhood. They've been through the fire, she says, and are toughened to life.

On the other hand Grimm says, "I've seen people who have had tremendous problems growing up, who by trial and error learned how to survive. But you have to be careful designating who is well-adjusted and who isn't. Someone may have had a rough childhood and be a high achiever. We don't see their pain. They may have a great need for control, but when they lose it, it makes them very vulnerable. They are brittle in their form of adjustment."

Some forms of covering up pain can be harmful. Since pain is nature's warning that something is wrong, those who feel less pain may not be aware of possible life-threatening symptoms. Denying pain also lowers the immune system because fewer cells are produced to fight infection, according to researcher and psychology professor Larry Jamner of California State University, San Bernardino.

Pain is emotional as well as physical, and usually produces anxiety. "People in pain who claim they're not feeling much anxiety actually experience more than they're aware of," says Jamner.

Further studies have indicated that people who feel less pain may produce more brain chemicals known as endorphins, which act like the opiates heroin and morphine. The chemical inhibits the transfer of information from one brain cell to another. When these pain messages are halted, the person feels no pain.

"What you learn from dealing with people in pain is that medication is not a long-term solution," says Wexler. "One has to learn to deal effectively with personal problems, to know the importance of keeping the muscles toned, to keep occupied in life, and to engage in interesting pursuits that divert one from a constant focus on pain."

Physical and psychological pain are mysterious companions. In some cases we must feel pain in order to be aware that something in our system is wrong. Then we must choose whether to let the pain force us into more misery, or rise above it and enhance our quality of life. As single women we may have the edge when it comes to handling pain, both physical and psychological, because we're used to leaning on ourselves.

Two Shadowy Words

Women will discuss everything from ingrown toenails to breast cancer, but rarely will they talk about urinary incontinence. Recent studies reveal that it affects more younger women than is commonly supposed. Thirty percent of those affected experience incontinence during exercise activities. The average age of those affected is under 39.

Many of these women acknowledge that they simply wear a sanitary pad during exercise, and a few report mild conditions to their physicians. The first time they sneeze and wet their pants, they may be surprised, but they keep it hidden and let the problem grow worse.

Single women who live alone find it easier to cover up the condition because no one is around to notice or to question them about it.

Too many women limit their activities instead of getting treatment, and this is the worst thing a single woman can do. Today a majority of women can be helped with behavior modification to relearn control of the bladder, or with exercises to firm up sagging pelvic muscles. Medication is given infrequently and surgery is considered a last resort.

Early awareness and knowledge are the best preventive

measures. Sixty percent of the time, incontinence is caused by omission of specific exercises following childbirth, lack of regular exercise, or obesity. The other 40 percent of the causes are related to diminished estrogen levels, problems with bladder function, infection or unknown causes.

Regardless of age or cause, incontinence can be cured or controlled for at least two-thirds of women (some doctors claim 95 percent). Recent studies show that treatment dramatically improves one's self-image.

Women of all ages can employ what are called Kegel exercises to strengthen pelvic muscles. It's a good idea to do these exercises *before* problems with incontinence begin. Simply focus on the muscle used to stop urination and then repeatedly contract and relax that muscle. A series of rapid contractions and relaxations can be done daily, followed by long contractions and relaxation. Some doctors recommend that those already suffering from incontinence should contract and relax the muscle for one minute every hour.

If you're involved in a sexual relationship, the exercise can be done during intercourse, probably much to the pleasure of your partner.

Another method being used is behavioral modification in which women learn how better to control their bladders.

"The basis for this approach is that continence is a learned procedure," says Arieh Bergman, M.D., associate professor of obstetrics and gynecology at the University of Southern California School of Medicine. "It's something that children master by the age of two or three. Some women may need to be re-educated. We're not sure why.

It could be that the neurological controls from the brain may weaken. They tell the bladder when it's time to void, rather than waiting for the bladder to tell them. At first a woman might void every hour. The goal is to void on command," says Bergman.

The preceding covers some of the major health concerns facing women today. The best way to enjoy good health is to take preventive measures. But there is a certain amount of illness we're going to have to contend with as we age, despite our miles of jogging, hours of aerobics, balanced diets, friendships, lovers, efforts to control anger, volunteer contributions, and optimism.

Like it or not, we all age, and personally I refuse to do it gracefully.

IX

Out and About

The Restaurant Business

Single women dining alone occasionally run into subtle hostility, especially if they don't want to sit at a luncheonette counter. All too often they're shunted to a dark corner by the restroom or kitchen door. Restaurant employees may act like there's something wrong with a woman who chooses to eat out alone, especially for an evening meal.

Sometimes I get the feeling that the staff feels sorry for or disturbed by a female solo diner. Many's the time I've eaten by myself while traveling by car, and small-town restaurants seem especially unaccustomed to women dining alone. I always learn more when I'm alone, however, such as how much the man sitting in the booth next to mine just won in Las Vegas. He's really laying it on to the waitress, which means he probably won back half of what he took with him.

There are a lot of people like myself who feel a pleasant restaurant is a great place to observe life. Natalie Goldberg in her book *Writing Down the Bones* devotes an entire chapter to the pleasure of writing in restaurants. However, she cautions writers not to show up with a notebook during lunch or dinner rush hours.

I work out of my home and sometimes miss the camaraderie of an office, and I'll often take my breaks in one of the little restaurants in the mountain community where I live. When I do that, it isn't just for the food. I like the noises in the kitchen and the chatter of the other patrons. I never fail to meet or hear someone interesting. I met two of the women I interviewed for this book at a local restaurant. One woman walked in with such a great smile on her face, and such a command of the atmosphere around her that I told the owner, "I'll bet that woman's single and has a story. I'd like to meet her." And that's how I came to know Glenna McAnish.

A few years ago I visited a friend who was going through a divorce after 19 years of marriage. She lived in a beautiful and lively area, so we set an itinerary: an elegant restaurant. Then she admitted that she'd never been to dinner in "that type of restaurant" without a man. I was thunderstruck, but talked her into going anyway. She was nervous the entire time, but said she knew she'd have to start getting used to it.

Because she had been insulated for so long, I explained to her how times have changed. Today it's nothing to see women eating together in any type of restaurant, nor to see one dining by herself.

Since the number of singles is growing so rapidly, and because singles aren't shy about eating out alone anymore, restaurants all over the country are working toward accommodating the single diner. Monty's Steak House in Westwood, California, has a plan for singles called "shared seating." Single patrons are asked if they'd like to sit with someone. Monty's customers have described it as a great way to avoid staring at the wallpaper. They've enjoyed meeting new faces over a meal. Shared seating isn't new in other parts of the world, but the concept is just gaining ground in the U.S.

Some restaurants have "maverick tables" where singles can sit together—an idea that originated in an Ann Landers column. A few restaurants have food bars where single patrons can gather. Some of the larger hotel chains set single tables to lure single travelers away from room service and into the dining room.

Bob Levey, writing in the *Washington Post*, told of a national restaurant chain that has set up "captain's tables" for singles, and a place in Chicago that serves singles at a table with family-style platters. Many restaurants, both independents and chains, are training their employees to be more sensitive to single diners.

Single diners used to be greeted by the hostess with "Dining alone?" then by the waiter, "Dining alone?" The question was really an implicit, "Gee, you going to take up all this space on your own?"

Restaurateur and designer Adam Tihany, who has designed such restaurants as Le Cirque, Bice, and Hubert's in Manhattan, as well as several in the Los Angeles area, pays special attention to accommodating singles, including movable tables for one or two, and upholstered sofas that run along the wall so that diners can face the room.

Tihany owns Remi, a restaurant on Manhattan's Upper East Side that encourages single diners to use the restaurant as a European-type cafe and bring reading material with them. "They're welcome to stay as long as they want to," he says.

"A typical problem of restaurants is that if they give up a table for a single person, they feel a bit of loss," he continues. "They can't make as much money serving a single at a table that would normally seat more. So we have developed a very comfortable bar area equipped to serve singles without making them feel like they are eating on a counter in a coffee shop. We offer comfortable seating, individual table settings and proper lighting.

"Most important, though, is proper attitude," Tihany says. "The staff is trained to make singles feel at home and the menus include dishes that lend themselves to smaller portions." Remi offers smaller bottles of wine for single diners.

Tihany acknowledges that it's easier to put restaurants that cater to singles in metropolitan areas with a lot of single traffic or near shopping centers and universities. "You wouldn't want to put one in a family-oriented community," he says. "It just wouldn't get enough single trade."

Restaurant owners in busy commercial business sections are very aware of the singles' crowd at lunch time. "That's why luncheonettes are so popular," he says. "There's a bit of psychology to the single diner. If they go out to eat, they usually don't want to sit there for hours, usually. They want to do it quickly and go back to work. Lots of single people don't go out to eat for entertainment."

Tihany has noted that Americans haven't taken to single dining like Europeans. Goldberg mentions in her book that writing in a Paris cafe is very acceptable, even expected. "You can order one coffee at 8:00 A.M. and still be sipping it with no pressure at 3:00 P.M." But in America, singles feel vulnerable. "They think it might translate into a pickup scene," says Tihany.

Tihany acknowledges that many restaurateurs are still

biased against single diners. He laughs and says it's not uncommon for singles to call and make a reservation for two and then when they get to the restaurant, to pretend that the other person simply didn't show up.

So, he says restaurants should design their places to accommodate singles. "Singles make steady clientele and loyal customers. We have a few at Remi who continually come in by themselves and they've managed to make good friends with the staff. When people are with someone, they talk with each other. When they come in by themselves they will talk to the staff."

At Sandro's, an Italian restaurant in New York, manager Gregory Adam says they had a communal table for singles, but it didn't work out. They still make special efforts to accommodate singles, however, because they cater to a large group of business people who are used to dining alone. Still, he says, "I'm single myself and I get 'that look' when I go into a nice restaurant. Fortunately, since I'm in the business myself I understand what they're saying. But my own staff is trained to be especially nice to singles."

Several restaurant owners say it just makes good business sense to be sensitive to the single diner because retail food competition makes it necessary. Stepp's in Los Angeles and Cutters in Santa Monica, California, were designed with single diners in mind by Restaurants Unlimited of Seattle, owner of 20 restaurants nationwide.

Rick Giboney, vice president of the marketing division of the company, says that singles like their style of restaurants not so much because they're dedicated to single diners, which they're not, but because they're "approachable" and "bright."

"People can go in and order anything anytime," he says.

"They can come in and have a dish of pasta, salad and a glass of wine at dinner time and feel welcome." The emphasis is on choice. Singles can choose to sit in the dining room at a single table, at the bar where food is served, or at the stand-up, waist-high tables that are considered "community tables."

"It isn't any one thing that draws singles to our places, as much as it is an attitude," Giboney says. "Singles don't want to feel conspicuous. They want to feel comfortable. They usually don't want a long, drawn-out meal with a lot of extraordinary service. Our places tend to look safe. They aren't dark. A single female can come in and not have vultures waiting."

Giboney says the company's restaurants aren't designed specifically for single women. "Women will feel comfortable. Men tend to be more tolerant of where they eat, but women want bright, cheery, stylish places that aren't heavily masculine."

Other restaurants, too, are making efforts to accommodate solo diners. Nicole's in Sacramento, California, has a communal table; Pava's in the same city has a raised counter-cum-wine bar where singles can eat; the Zuni Cafe, located in downtown San Francisco, provides a table for one that's always occupied and that sends the message that singles are welcome, and Town and Country Village in Sacramento offers magazines and newspapers for their single diners to read. Some feature theme nights, such as the Rhinoceros in Detroit's Rivertown section which offers an "Ain't Nothin' but a Divorce" party from 4:00 P.M. until 8:00 P.M. on Sundays.

Other restaurateurs have tried new concepts for singles, but have failed. Leon's Restaurant Services of North Plainfield, New Jersey, tried fostering the idea of Friendship

Tables throughout the country a few years ago. Owner Morris Egert says he came up with the idea when a friend of his, a pilot, who sometimes had short stopovers, said it would be nice if he could share meals. Egert established Friendship Tables on his own and then offered other restaurants promotional materials to get started, but the idea didn't catch on, he says.

Hotel dining rooms are also getting into the act. Nick Hill of Marriott Hotels talks about the chain's solo dining concepts in many of their 220 main-line hotels. These include the placement of a centrally located television, reading materials and good reading light in their restaurants. "We don't want them to stay in their rooms," Hill says. "The special accommodations eliminate intimidation of our solo guests."

Part of the new accommodations for travelers result from the fact that they have so many more business clients now, many of whom are women.

Marriott, like many other hotel chains, has upgraded facilities to cater to the needs of women travelers, offering hair dryers, hangers for women's suits and dresses, full-length mirrors, ironing boards and irons, lighted mirrors, and vanities, according to Hill. "We've also upgraded our door locks so women can feel more secure."

At the Albuquerque Hilton, a floor dedicated to single women travelers has been a big hit. Only women were allowed when it first opened, but because it was often not completely occupied, males were allowed to book rooms if the hotel is full. Director of Marketing Russell Archuleta says it offers upgraded security, mirrors, hair dryers, dried flower arrangements and plusher towels. The Albuquerque hotel also offers special dining services to singles in a dining area called the Rancher's Club of New Mexico.

Other trends indicating that more singles will be eating out alone include the dining habits reported by the U.S. Department of Agriculture's Human Nutrition Information Service: (1) Americans, excluding those who live in institutions, eat more than one of five meals away from home; (2) fast-food restaurants serve four out of 10 meals eaten away from home; (3) four of 10 consumers say they have changed their eating-out habits to reflect nutrition concerns; (4) adults eat roughly 30 percent of their calories away from home; (5) Americans spend more than 40 cents of every food dollar on food eaten away from home.

Good news about eating alone is that researchers at Georgia State University in Atlanta have found that people tend to eat almost twice as much when they dine in social situations as when they eat alone.

In order to maintain healthful eating habits when dining out, the USDA recommends that you do the following:

—Order steamed seafood, raw vegetables, or fruit as appetizers and go easy on rich sauces, dips and batter-fried foods.

—Order a cup of soup rather than a bowl and ask for broth- or tomato-base soups rather than creamed types.

—Choose meat, fish or poultry that is broiled, grilled, baked, steamed or poached rather than fried. The USDA recommends that you ask to have your entree prepared without added fat.

—Select lean cuts of meat in place of prime rib or spareribs, and trim away visible fat.

—Ask for a take-home bag when the meat portion is much more than three ounces.

—Check to see if half-portions are available.

—Order an appetizer rather than an entree as your main course.
—Choose dishes flavored with herbs and spices rather than with rich sauces, gravies or dressings.
—Try stir-fried mixtures prepared with little oil.
—Consider vegetable toppings such as onions and green peppers when ordering pizza.
—Go easy on the dressing when ordering salad or preparing your own at a salad bar.
—When eating at a deli, choose lean meats such as turkey or ham instead of fat cold cuts like bologna or salami.
—Choose fruits or sherbets (over ice cream) when ordering desserts.

Other tips for dining out healthfully include the following:

—When ordering cocktails, choose sparkling water with a twist of lime, fruit juice cocktail or wine spritzer.
—Appetizers can be a melon wedge, fruit medley, gazpacho or shrimp cocktail.
—Salads might consist of fresh fruit, garden pasta or seafood.
—Healthy entrees include baked chicken breast, beef *en brochette*, burritos, pasta primavera or a small steak.
—Great veggies to order are herbed new potatoes, sliced tomatoes, zucchini and carrots, peas with pearl onions or corn-on-the-cob (but watch the butter).

For those who enjoy truly fine dining but feel uncomfortable alone in a plush restaurant, the Single Gourmet, a nationwide dining organization for singles, has 21 chapters and nearly 3,000 members of all ages. Spokeswoman Aileen Haskell emphasizes that the organization isn't a dating service. "There's no matchmaking," she says. "It's purely a social dining club. Everything we do focuses around dining. We provide lovely dinner parties at top restaurants. People want to be good to themselves on occasion. Sometimes it's no fun eating alone, and in the better restaurants, singles sometimes aren't treated too well."

All outings are centered around dining and have included travel to China, Paris and Alaska. For further information on the Single Gourmet, write to them at 33 E. 58th St., New York, New York, 10022, or call (212) 980-8788.

Peregrinations

Women have become more adventuresome. They know there's an entire world out there waiting for them.

This short section on travel will neglect the usual travel cruises and trips where the idea is to hook up with some man. For women who choose to be single, travel has its own rewards. Besides, traveling on your own opens doors not available to couples.

The doors are opening wider today because traveling solo is in. New as well as established touring companies are reaching out to the singles who aren't interested in the traditional cruise where people sit lined up in lounge chairs and commiserate with one another.

Many hotels now bend over backwards for singles, although there is still price discrimination (see chapter 4). Touring and travel companies are offering singles everything from white-water rafting to archeological dig vacations.

A person's social life is often richer because of her single status, and so are her travel options. You simply have the chance to meet more diverse people if you're single and traveling.

When Rebecca Kuzins toured New Orleans alone she was invited into the homes of many families she met along the way. She was taken to several out-of-the-way places she wouldn't otherwise have had the opportunity to see. When Kuzins travels, she's looking for experiences, not men.

The first trip I took completely by myself was a two-week stint to Cody, Wyoming, and Yellowstone National Park. I trooped around by bus, on foot and on horse, stayed in a variety of cabins and lodges and ate all my meals in restaurants. But I never ate alone because I never failed to meet interesting people, some foreign, who had come to explore those same areas. They would spy me standing alone in line, or at a table, and ask me to dine with them. I enjoyed myself immensely and learned a lot about other cultures to boot.

I did a great deal of hiking and walking, including a 10-mile walk outside Cody, where I met a wonderful woman, who with her husband ran a small museum. I sat by a wood stove, and visited with her for a few hours, learning the history of the place, how she and her husband had hauled logs down from two old log cabins and reassembled them to make their present home and museum.

When you're traveling with a man, you're more likely to limit your discussions with strangers. Some single women say their ex-husbands complained when they struck up conversations with strangers they didn't know. Nor do single women necessarily want to travel with another woman unless they know her travel style. Most prefer traveling companions who don't demand to do everything together. I happen to like to walk and hike on trips. One of the friends I often travel with doesn't like to walk a lot. Most of the day we each go our separate ways, meeting for things we both enjoy. On the other hand, I've known many solo travelers who have made lifetime friends of people they've met on tours and trips.

The opportunities can be endless for the solo traveler, and are available for those with the means. I've known women lacking funds for travel who tie travel in with their work, or who exchange services for places to stay, or who even exchange their homes in order to get a look at another part of the country. It's only one's imagination that holds one back from getting involved in an adventure.

Here are parts of a letter about travel and adventure from Betty Wold. This woman finds adventure everywhere she goes. She can serve as a model to us all.

"In August I drove to Chicago to pick up Mary, and we headed for Erie for our 50th high school class reunion. It was really great. My favorite teacher, Mr. Vivian Marion Lewis, was there, still hale and hearty. Plays golf every day and still teaches at a junior college. Said he was delighted to see that so many of us were healthy enough to want to come and wealthy enough to be able to.

"After the reunion weekend we went to Wattsburg and spent four days at a terrific ski resort owned by a good friend of Dodie's and now a friend to all of us. Can't say much for the skiing in Erie in August but the blackberry picking was perfect.

"Spent two lively days in Akron with Beazie and Al. . . . Then on to New Wilmington for a fine stay with my cousins, Virginia and Bill.

"Uneventful but beautiful trip home through West Virginia, Kentucky, Missouri and Arkansas. I read someplace recently that by 2010, 95 percent of all Americans will live within 50 miles of either coast. They simply won't know what they are missing!

"Was home four days, then to the Ozark Folk Center in Arkansas to give a demonstration on making rose beads and also to have a booth at their craft fair. . . .

"The following week I was invited to an author's party in Joplin. Said I still lacked two chapters in my book, but they said, 'Come anyway and take advance orders . . .'

"Really did want to have it finished before I went to New Zealand, but I guess I just can't play so much and work too.

"About New Zealand. Kath has made the most wonderful plans for me while I am there. I will visit every mile of both islands and the lovely part is that I will meet real people, not just more tourists. I will be met in Auckland by herb-lovers who will eventually hand me down to Christ Church on time for their convention. . . .

"I'm going to intimidate some travel agents tomorrow and see if I can route myself so that I leave from Tulsa, with a stopover in Phoenix, then home by way of Sacramento and Denver. I don't know if that is possible, but I'll have a go at it and see what I can jack up."

Exchange Clubs

Through an exchange club you list your home in an exchange club directory, and use that same directory to locate a home in the area you want to visit.

Exchange clubs allow you to get to know an area better, perhaps with longer stays. They place you in the culture of the area, provide an inexpensive home base for short trips and allow you to visit relatives without imposing on them.

Through exchange club listings, you can offer to exchange with someone who will use your home while you occupy theirs; you can rent rooms while you remain in your home; members of your family (particularly teens) can exchange with another person for a cross-cultural experience; and house-sitting opportunities are made available.

Other services can be offered or rendered through the exchange clubs. All have a modest fee for listing your requests, and business is conducted directly with the other listed person or persons and not through the exchange club, which holds no responsibility.

For further information contact:
Vacation Exchange Club
12006 111th Ave.
Youngtown, AZ 85363
1-602-972-2186

Another source is the Traveler's Information Exchange, established in 1891 as the Women's Rest Tour Association. This organization has enabled thousands of people who love to travel to share their experiences with others. Considered one of the oldest travel clubs in the United States, it was originally an all-female organization established expressly to provide women with solo vacations.

Jan Stankus of the Traveler's Information Exchange explains that TIE was founded in 1891 by a small group of women who refused to accept the norm of the day that women had to travel with chaperones. They started what was basically an underground travelers' organization for adventurous women. They had to pledge that they would never show their lodging lists or other information to anyone who was not a member, including their husbands. The organization's first president was Julia Ward Howe, composer of "Battle Hymn of the Republic."

Today, men can join TIE, but the majority of members (about 500 nationwide) are women. Many are seniors who are widowed or who have never married.

Stankus, 42, has never married and lives alone. "I'm probably a good example of the type of person you are planning to profile," she says. "When I travel, I prefer to get involved in some sort of educational venture." She has studied Greek in Greece, Arabic in Egypt, Portuguese in Brazil, and Italian in Italy. She has also participated in an Earthwatch expedition and an archaeological dig on the island of Menorca, Spain. "Situations like these allow me to get involved with the country I'm visiting in a way that is not accessible to a 'tourist,' yet allows me to stay somewhat independent without feeling lonely," she says. "There are some terrific people who get involved in travel-and-learn experiences and I've made some good friends as a result."

Membership, which costs $25, includes a newsletter of travel tips, an annual magazine that contains accounts of members' travel adventures, and lists of accommodations and restaurants all over the world that members have recommended. It also provides some discounts for particular services and eligibility to participate in the organization's own bed-and-breakfast exchange program.

Traveler's Information Exchange
356 Boylston St.
Boston, MA 02166
1-617-536-5651

For those of you looking for a different sort of exchange, there is the Friendship Force, a non-profit, non-political organization that provides a quality cross-cultural, educational living experience for people around the globe.

People who travel under the auspices of the Friendship Force are home-hosted for one to two week periods, allowing time to get to know a country and its people with the help of the hosts.

The organization was founded by former missionary Wayne Smith and former president Jimmy Carter and his wife in an effort to improve international relations through establishment of international friendships.

Applicants must qualify for the program, since it is geared to those who find the differences between people intriguing. It's for those who can adapt wholeheartedly to an environment and lifestyle different from their own.

Those who are accepted into the program may serve as ambassadors or hosts. There is an induction fee which covers the cost of the exchange experience, including international transportation and a week's home hosting.

More than a million people in 40 countries have participated in the Friendship Force.

The Friendship Force
575 South Tower, One CNN Center
Atlanta, GA 30303 USA
1-404-522-9490

Loners on Wheels and Loners of America are two RV or travel-trailer organizations geared toward singles. Loners on Wheels is for singles only. Men and women traveling as couples aren't eligible for membership. Members must travel in their own units. They receive a newsletter listing upcoming rallies throughout the country at a variety of campsites. Also, members can contact one another for travel companions for self-planned trips. Chapters exist throughout the United States and Canada.

The newsletter also prints "tidbits" in its Mail Call column. A few examples: A member from Canada says she'll be gone for the summer but anyone stopping by her place on the Trans-Canada Highway can use the facilities at her home. Another tells how her rig was stolen in a parking lot and she lost all the addresses of her LW friends. She's asking members to send her their addresses.

One man who had traveled with the group for years wrote to thank them for all the fun he'd had. Said he'd miss it all, but he's dying of cancer. He'd known about his condition for some time but continued traveling with them rather than spend time taking chemotherapy treatments. He wrote a poem with the theme, "See you UP the road."

Lorraine Shannon, vice president of Loners of America says that LOA was organized in 1987 by a group of RV-ers who felt the need for a member-owned-and-operated club for singles only. It now has 1,400 members and 30 chapters throughout the United States.

Many LOA members are full-timers who live year-round in their recreational vehicles, heading south in the winter and north in the summer. Approximately 75 percent are women, and about that same number are retired or semi-retired.

Campouts are usually informal social gatherings but rallies are more structured and last nearly a week. Planned activities include games, skits, lectures, organized meals and tours. Line-dancing has become popular with the singles' group because it requires no partner, Shannon says.

Loners on Wheels
P.O. Box 1355
Poplar Bluff, MO 63901

Loners of America
Rt. 2, Box 85E
Elsinor, MO 63937

American Wilderness Experience president Dave Wiggins says his organization has been tracking the growth in the number of single women taking wilderness trips. In 1988 it was about 32 percent and in 1989 it was more than 34 percent. Average age of their female guests is between 30 to 45, but he's noticed in the past few years that the number of women over 60 is increasing.

The AWP has been operating for 20 years and is recognized as the largest domestic adventure travel company. It serves as a broker and central reservations service to professional backcountry guides, outfitters and guest ranches throughout the United States, and also sells directly to the public.

American Wilderness Experience
P.O. Box 1486
Boulder, CO 80306
1-303-444-2632
or 1-800-494-2996

Youth hostels in Europe have nothing on senior hosteling, a program for those over 60 that combines travel and learning experiences, plus inexpensive accommodations. Elderhostel, a travel/study program headquartered in Boston and begun in 1975, has served hundreds of thousands of seniors who have traveled and studied in 42 countries, taking courses ranging from zoology to sports. The program, which houses seniors in college dorms and provides meals and other activities, usually spans six days and requires no homework or grades.

It consists of a network of more than 1,500 colleges, universities, environmental education centers, youth hostels, museums and other educational and cultural institutions which offer low-cost, short-term, residential aca-

demic programs for adults who are 60 and older. Programs are offered in the United States and Canada and in more than 40 countries overseas. In 1989 more than 190,000 people enrolled in its programs, up from about 160,000 the previous year. Participants can now travel in their own recreational vehicles or in transportation provided by the host institution. One example: A combination floating-and-terrestrial trek in which hostelers followed the 1898 goldrush trail to the Klondike. The Klondike trek was sponsored by the University of Alaska.
Elderhostel
60 Boylston St., Suite 400
Boston, MA 02116
1-617-426-7788

Bikecentennial provides a magazine, yellow pages and other sources and guidebooks, such as a state-by-state listing of 140 U.S. bicycle tour operators and maps of the U.S. National Bicycle Trails Network.
Bikecentennial
P.O. Box 8308-PF
Missoula, MT 59807

American Youth Hostels. Members of any age may use youth hostels throughout the world and receive the brochure "World Adventure Travel Program," in addition to participation in local AYH bicycle tours.
AYH National Office
Marketing Information Dept.
P.O. Box 37613
Washington, DC 20013-7613

There are, of course, hundreds of other organizations and travel agencies that can offer the single traveler her choice of where and how she wants to travel. The above groups have been mentioned only to illustrate that we don't have to limit ourselves to traditional tours and cruise-ship vacations. It's nice to have money to travel, but wealth isn't necessary if you tap into some of the agencies mentioned.

For further listings and information contact a local travel agency, ask for travel reference books at the library, study your Sunday newspaper's travel section, attend travel lectures and listen to friends and acquaintances tell of their travel exploits.

X

Epilogue

My friend Haila who is an authority on symbolism and mythology, both Eastern and New Age, called me recently from her home in Idaho. We argued about the truth behind the choice to be single. She asked if I truly believed what I was writing; she had the notion that I was writing about the advantages of singlehood over marriage.

I tried to assure her that choosing one over the other wasn't the intent of my book—that living fully and to the maximum, whatever a person's marital status, was the goal.

I tried to explain to her, as I've tried to explain to my readers, that women need to feel complete within themselves whether they are married or single and that finding Mr. Right isn't going to make any woman feel whole. I often remind myself that some married women believe their lives would be better if they were single, and some single women believe they would be better off married.

Both ways of thinking are lies. We're better off only when we realize that no outside force is going to make us happy. Living happily ever after is an American myth. Haila agrees that happily-ever-after is the stuff of fairy tales, but wonders if I've lost the ability to compromise in order to make a relationship work.

The answer is, of course, I realize it takes compromise to make a relationship work. It also takes compromise to be single. It takes compromise simply to live. Our lives are full of choices and compromises. Despite what *Cosmopolitan* editor Helen Gurley Brown says, we *can't* have it all.

Still, writing this book has caused me to change some of the attitudes I held at the onset. That's good, because there is no real learning without confrontation. Haila's comments made me delve even deeper into what I had learned from my research. She's good at rattling my cage, and that's okay. She and I both know it's important to look past the obvious when we're studying something.

Writing this book made me realize that I was ready to be confronted, and ready to find out exactly why it feels so good and so right to be single. Some of my questions were answered as I interviewed other women. I had been put off by the countless number of books that tell women —that exhort women—to get out there and find a man whatever the cost. These books perpetuate the lie that all women want and need to be living with a male, and that any sort of relationship is better than none.

The truths I have had to face are: (1) sometimes I'm lonely; (2) sometimes I think I'm missing out on something (I don't know quite what but feel it anyway); (3) when I come in late at night to a cold house I wish I had someone to talk to besides the dog; (4) I sometimes worry about growing old alone; (5) I sometimes wish there were a man around to fix the dripping faucet; (6) I miss having a warm body next to me in bed.

I've lived long enough, and am experienced enough, however, to know that (1) many women who are married feel lonely at times; (2) everyone, married or single, sometimes feels they're missing out on something (but don't quite know what); (3) sometimes when you're married you may come home and have someone to talk to, but the talk is often an argument, complaint or demand; (4) there's a good chance a woman is going to grow old alone anyway since women tend to outlive men; (5) some men aren't any better at fixing plumbing than women, plus they might fix the drip, but you may still be stuck with washing, ironing, and preparing the meals; (6) if I want a warm body next to mine I can get one—but do I really want it? Sex can be dangerous and not only for single women. Some married women have contracted AIDS from their husbands.

So my basic premise hasn't changed. Staying single or marrying are choices and they both involve compromise. One thing is paramount, however: Women do have more of a choice today than ever before. It's easier for us to choose to be single. We don't have to settle for less just to get married, and this may be both a bane and a bonus. The women interviewed for this book come from all walks of life. Most love men, have loved men, and will continue to love them even though they choose to live alone.

Their reasons for remaining single are as varied as their lives. I acknowledged to Haila, "Yes, if I happened to meet a man with whom I wanted to spend my life, and who I thought would complement my life, I might latch onto him." But because I'm relatively content with my life as it is (though I'd like to travel more and have more money and buy my friends and relatives more gifts than I can now afford), I'm not out there wasting time and energy looking.

The ideas I live with now, however, have never been planted in cement. They are rooted in the earth and subject to growth.

Soon after my divorce nearly 12 years ago, I told a therapist that I would never remarry. He told me not to play God. So I don't try to play one of the gods when I write.

I talk about change, about choice and diversity. Ideas about love change with the ages and with age. It's wonderful to be wildly, madly, erotically in love. It's also great to have a quiet, still love that causes little anxiety.

Some truths about singlehood are self-evident. The longer one has been single, the more likely she is to remain so. Single women develop a certain hardiness that helps keep them healthy in old age. Some, however, would like to live with a man, or marry one, if they could find a suitable match. But they say it's difficult to find a man who's worth giving up what they've established for themselves.

All of these findings point to the two major concepts of this book, which are: healthy single women are complete in themselves; and being single can be a healthy way to live. The former is disputed by my friend Haila. She believes in the tradition of complements—that both men and women are lacking and that when joined together they make a complete entity.

She explains that within all males there are some female qualities and vice versa, and that complementary opposites are in contrast but not conflict, and this contrast is what complements and eventually brings about harmony. I know these things already, but I don't believe they mean a woman has to live with a man to live in harmony.

I believe the traditions, religions and mythologies that illustrate the relationship between the yin and yang are beautiful, and helpful. These stories move us beyond, and even in a different direction from pure biology, which compels male and female to procreate. All one has to do is look around to know there are plenty of people doing a damn fine job at continuing the species. Many of the single women written about on these pages have had children.

Still, at some point in our lives, it must be okay to decide to be single. Perhaps a husband has died, as was the case with several of the women I interviewed. Or a long-term marriage was ended. A few of my interviewees had never been married, but said they would if they could meet the right man, and a few others said they wouldn't marry under any circumstances.

Haila wondered if the choice to remain single wasn't linked to selfishness. "Have you reached a point where you can't give and take, where you can't sacrifice a little to have a relationship?" she asked.

My answer to her is, "Why should being in a relationship have to sound so bleak?"

I have married friends who have chosen not to have children. Some of them have been accused of selfishness. To the people who make those accusations, I ask, "Where did these people ever get the idea that *having* children was unselfish?"

When we become parents we do it to fulfill our own needs, so having children could be construed as being selfish. Naturally you make sacrifices when you are a parent—from birth onward. But the joys outweigh the sacrifice or people wouldn't continue to do it.

It's the same with relationships. When the pain and sacrifice of marriage outweigh the pleasure of staying single, why would a rational woman choose the former?

Once again, the subject boils down to choice. Women should have the option of remaining single without being told subtly or outright that they're incomplete if they're not part of a couple. A woman of any age shouldn't feel compelled to sap her energy looking for a man when she could be using that power to make her life more fulfilling and dynamic. That's not to say she might not meet a man and change her mind. But why must she put her life on hold in the meantime?

Why should meeting a man be the priority of her life when there's an entire world out there teeming with satisfying causes, work and play? You will note that I haven't said that single women are always happy. Happiness is something that comes to people occasionally. Anyone, married or single, who's happy all the time has to be a fool.

Another friend, a mother of grown children and single for about 15 years, recently wrote me a letter. We'd been trying to get together for several months for a weekend of cross-country skiing but hadn't found a time that worked for both of us.

For the past seven years or so, this woman had been deeply involved with a man. They had met on a ski trip, and subsequently skied all over the world as a couple. They shared many favorite pastimes such as hiking, gourmet cooking, theater, music, and they spent considerable time together—sometimes weeks at a time—while maintaining their individual residences.

They had recently broken up, however, because she refused to marry him. It was a tough decision for her because she knew it meant the end of their relationship. Soon after their breakup, he informed my friend that he had met another woman and they were planning to marry.

My friend was clearly distraught, but knew her decision was the right one. She had weighed the pros and cons of marriage to him and had decided that she was better off single. Although she knew they shared many things in common, mostly activities, their values, political beliefs and other mundane likes and dislikes were quite different. When she has time off from her job she's used to catching a plane to New York at the drop of a hat to visit her daughter and granddaughter and attend the theater. If she wants to take off for a long walk on the beach near her home, she can do so any time of day or night without checking in with someone first. She's free to buy what she wants with her own money without asking permission, and to invite weekend guests without consulting a partner. I'm sure she thought of all of these things, and many others, when she was making her decision.

As single women, we weigh and evaluate all the time. If at some point in our lives we believe that living with someone would add to our lives, rather than detract, then we would be women who choose not to be single.

Haila would agree with that. She met and is married to a man who complements her. She wouldn't have settled for any less, and I'm happy for her.

A growing number of us, however, are women who choose to be single. And we believe that, temporarily or permanently, the choice is the best one for us. We're willing to accept the consequences of our actions—both the joy and the sadness. We simply believe that by being single right now, the scales are tipped in our favor.

Bibliography

Adams, Margaret, *Single Blessedness*, Basic Books, New York, 1978.

Brown, Gabrielle, *The New Celibacy*, McGraw-Hill, New York, 1980.

Business Week, March 5, 1990, p. 20.

Buxton, Amity Pierce, *The Other Side of the Closet*. IBS Press, Santa Monica, California, 1990.

Chambers-Schiller, Lee Virginia, *Liberty, A Better Husband: Single Women in America, The Generations of 1789–1840*, Yale University Press, New Haven and London, 1984.

Cillins, Emily, *The Whole Single Person's Catalog*, Peebles Press, New York and London, 1979.

Cockrum, Janet and White, Priscilla, "Influences on the Life Satisfaction of Never-Married Men and Women," *Family Relations: Journal of Applied Family and Child Studies* 34(1985):551–556.

Ellis, Robert, *Anger, How to Live with and without It*, Citadel Press, New Jersey, 1983.

Frachhia, Charles A., *How to Be Single Creatively*, McGraw-Hill, New York, 1979.

Goldberg, Natalie, *Writing Down the Bones*, Shambhala, Boston and London, 1986.

Hibbard, Judith H., Schmoldt, Ralph A. and Pope, Clyde R., "Marital Interaction and the Health and Well-Being of Spouses," *Women & Health* 15(1989):35–54.

Jong, Erica, *Any Woman's Blues*, Harper & Rowe, New York, 1990.
Journal of Gerontology, "Medical Sciences, AIDS and the Elderly," May 1990.
Kraft, William F., *Sexual Dimensions of the Celibate Life*, Andrews & McMeel, Kansas City, 1979.
Large, Tom, "Some Aspects of Loneliness in Families," *Family Process* 28(1989):28-35.
Lenardon, Robert J. and Morford, Mark P. O., *Classical Mythology*, David McKay Company, New York, 1971.
Man Suffocated By Potatoes, ed. William A. Marsano, Signet, 1987.
Publiesi, Karen, "Employment Characteristics, Social Support and the Well-Being of Women," *Women & Health* 14(1988):35-54.
Richmond, Gary, *The Divorce Decision*, Word Book Publisher, Texas, 1988.
Rokach, Ami, "The Experience of Loneliness: A Tri-Level Model," *Journal of Psychology* 122(1988):531-541.
Savage, Terry, *Terry Savage Talks Money*, Dearborn Financial Publishing, Illinois, 1990.
Showalter, Elaine, *Sexual Anarchy*, Viking-Penguin, New York, 1990.
Stuewe-Portnoff, Greg, "Loneliness: Lost in the Landscape of Meaning," *Journal of Psychology* 122(1988):545-555.
Wolff, Bernard Pierre, *Friends and Friends of Friends*, Dutton, New York, 1978.